STRATEGIC PROJECT ANALYSIS

The forming, funding, approval, and planning of a project are key factors in its future success or failure. This book explains the use of strategic project analysis, and advocates for a closer relationship between economic analysis and project evaluation and provides real-world examples of major projects that have used this method.

The primary quantitative method for decision-making in project selection is cost-benefit analysis. However, the method has well-known flaws and challenges. Using the principles of stakeholders, risk, ethics, and bias, the book presents a rationale for broadening traditional project analysis to include both quantitative and qualitative methods. The identification of sustainability and resilience benefits and hidden value are highlighted as an equally important factor in assessing projects.

Written in a clear and accessible style with straightforward maths, this book is invaluable to project owners, decision-makers, and management professionals seeking broader tools to evaluate strategic projects, as well as students of project management.

Alexia Nalewaik is the owner of Pellucid Projects LLC and occasionally an adjunct professor in engineering economics and project evaluation at higher education institutions such as George Washington University and American University. She is a quantity surveyor with over 30 years of experience in audit, risk analysis, and cost management for complex capital mega-programs. She is a Fellow of RICS, AACE International, the Guild of Project Controls, and ICEC. She serves on RICS Governing Council and is a Past Chair of ICEC and a Past President of AACE International. This is her third book.

I0894620

"Nalewaik is an internationally renowned academic and practitioner in the art and science of project management, project controls, and governance, who has the breadth of knowledge, experience, and character to impart both soft and hard skills to those who have been fortunate enough to attend her lectures and presentations, as well as read her books and the important publications to which she has made significant contributions.

This book is essential reading for anyone concerned with establishing the groundwork for a successful project. Nalewaik delves into the early stages of the project lifecycle, when the project begins as little more than an idea, and its costs and benefits must be identified and articulated clearly in a competitive environment to get the necessary investment and gain support to proceed with execution and delivery. The text has a strategic focus throughout. Balancing the explanation of a variety of analytical and economic methodologies and models with the critical importance of human factors offers acceptable situations for their implementation as well as potential hurdles and restrictions."

Shane Forth, *Principal Consultant, Go Forth, UK*

"*Strategic Project Analysis* sheds light on the challenges of cost-benefit analysis during the fuzzy project front-end stage. The book provides a comprehensive and practical guide, covering critical and diverse topics, such as evaluation, planning, benefits, risk, stakeholders, project ownership, bias, and ethics. I highly recommend this as a guidebook to support managers in enhancing project investment decision-making."

Ofer Zwikael, *Professor, The Australian National University Canberra, Australia*

STRATEGIC PROJECT ANALYSIS

A POWERFUL SET OF COST-BENEFIT TOOLS AND TECHNIQUES FOR MANAGERS

Alexia Nalewaik

Routledge
Taylor & Francis Group
LONDON AND NEW YORK

Designed cover image: Getty Images

First published 2025
by Routledge
4 Park Square, Milton Park, Abingdon, Oxon OX14 4RN

and by Routledge
605 Third Avenue, New York, NY 10158

Routledge is an imprint of the Taylor & Francis Group, an informa business

British Library Cataloguing-in-Publication Data
A catalogue record for this book is available from the British Library

Library of Congress Cataloging-in-Publication Data
Names: Nalewaik, Alexia, author.
Title: Strategic project analysis : a powerful set of cost-benefit tools and techniques for managers / Alexia Nalewaik.
Description: Abingdon, Oxon ; New York, NY : Routledge, 2025. | Includes bibliographical references and index.
Identifiers: LCCN 2024025570 (print) | LCCN 2024025571 (ebook) | ISBN 9780367857639 (hardback) | ISBN 9781032874500 (paperback) | ISBN 9781003014928 (ebook)
Subjects: LCSH: Project management. | Project management—Evaluation. | Strategic planning.
Classification: LCC HD69.P75 N363 2025 (print) | LCC HD69.P75 (ebook) | DDC 658.4/04–dc23/eng/20240613
LC record available at https://lccn.loc.gov/2024025570
LC ebook record available at https://lccn.loc.gov/2024025571

ISBN: 978-0-367-85763-9 (hbk)
ISBN: 978-1-032-87450-0 (pbk)
ISBN: 978-1-003-01492-8 (ebk)

DOI: 10.4324/9781003014928

Typeset in Bembo
by Apex CoVantage, LLC

This book is dedicated to Kenneth King Humphreys (1938–2023)

CONTENTS

FIGURES

TABLES

EQUATIONS

FOREWORD

Although much has been written about decision-making in the realm of major companies, nonprofit organizations, and governments, as well as about the mathematical methods used to perform cost-benefit analysis (CBA) in terms of numerical results, this subject continues to be somewhat confusing - even embarrassing - to a great number of managers and analysts who need to select a project from a range of options and to commit themselves to allocate resources in its planning and execution phases.

One of the greatest challenges facing practitioners of CBA is the assessment of economic outcomes at the project's front-end stage. Here, uncertainty reigns supreme, casting a shadow over even the most meticulously crafted analyses. It is in these moments of ambiguity that the true value of CBA shines brightest, offering a structured framework to navigate the fog of uncertainty.

In her third book, *Strategic Project Analysis: A Powerful Set of Cost-Benefit Tools and Techniques for Managers*, Dr. Alexia Nalewaik's efforts fall on providing managers with a clear explanation of the art of selecting the most suitable method, evaluating its pros and cons, running the calculations, and interpreting the results, thus leading to a higher chance of success in the project outcome. This book serves as a beacon for sailors in turbulent seas of strategic decisions, offering robust cost-benefit analysis tools that light the way for managers and decision-makers. Through a pragmatic approach, *Strategic Project Analysis* delves into the heart of strategic project analysis, demystifying complexities and presenting alternative and complementary methods to traditional cost-benefit analysis.

The book kicks off with a critical discussion on CBA, pointing out its well-known flaws and challenges. This section elucidates the need for alternative methods that address the intricacies inherent in project evaluation.

The author then proposes complementary approaches to traditional cost-benefit analysis, advocating for a closer relationship with project evaluation. This segment is enriched with real-world examples demonstrating the applicability of these alternative methodologies across various project contexts.

In its most innovative and attractive feature (at least to me, who deal with decision-making processes almost daily), the chapters about principles of stakeholders, risk, ethics, and bias emphasize the importance of considering a broader range of factors in project analysis, going beyond objective and mathematical approaches, to include stakeholders mapping, risk assessment, ethical considerations, and the recognition of a number of cognitive biases, thus significantly enriching strategic project analysis. Developing an awareness of ethical issues and recognizing personal and organizational biases are fundamental for a more objective and fair analysis. This involves constantly questioning one's assumptions and seeking a balanced understanding of the different perspectives involved.

Finally, upon shedding light on the most common blind spots in project analysis, the author tackles the issues of the underestimation of complexity and uncertainties associated. There's a tendency to overly rely on quantitative data, while critical qualitative factors such as the social impact of the project, ethical considerations, and stakeholder dynamics are overlooked.

Strategic Project Analysis is a book well worth reading and keeping on the table. It can be useful as technical literature, and as a source of theoretical and practical references, but its most valuable characteristics is to explain CBA in a language accessible to project managers in all levels of seniority, and to present the usually cumbersome mathematical models with eloquent examples, in a way that the reader will certainly become abler to take decisions in any field and industry in both public and private sectors.

Aldo Mattos
Owner, Aldo Mattos Consulting

ACKNOWLEDGMENTS

I would like to express sincere appreciation to all the friends and colleagues who provided advice and assistance, especially those who volunteered to critique (Morrie, Tony, Diane, David, and Jerry). I also give special thanks to Routledge for their unflagging patience.

ACRONYMS AND ABBREVIATIONS

AOA	analysis of alternatives
ASCE	American Society of Civil Engineers
BA	business analysis
BCA	benefit-cost analysis
BCR	benefit-cost ratio
BI	broader impacts
CBA	cost-benefit analysis
CCA	cost-consequence analysis
CEA	cost-effectiveness analysis
CUA	cost-utility analysis
DCFRR	discounted cash flow rate of return
DDE	doctrine of double effect
EA	economic analysis
EIA	Economic impact analysis
EIR	Environmental impact report
EPA	Environmental Protection Agency (United States)
ETPS	economic, technical, political, and social
FV	future value
GAM	goals achievement matrix
GAO	Government Accountability Office (United States)
GR&A	ground rules and assumptions
IE	impact evaluation
IEEE	Institute of Electrical and Electronics Engineers
IGO	intergovernmental organization
IRR	internal rate of return
LCCA	lifecycle cost analysis
LCCB	lifecycle cost-benefit analysis

LCCE	lifecycle cost estimate
LEED	Leadership in Energy and Environmental Design
MAC	marginal abatement cost
MACRS	modified accelerated cost recovery system
MARR	minimum acceptable rate of return
MCA	multi-criteria analysis
MoSCoW	Must or Should, Could or Would
NGO	non-governmental organization
NPV	net present value
NRAO	National Radio Astronomy Observatory
NSF	National Science Foundation
OBE	objectives-based evaluation
OMB	Office of Management and Budget (United States)
OPEX	operating expenditures
OR	operations research
PBS	planned balance sheet
PEST	political, economic, social, and technological
PESTEL	political, economic, social, technological, environmental, and legal
PI	profitability index
PIR	profit investment ratio
PMI	Project Management Institute
POPE	post-opening project evaluation
PPAR	project performance assessment report
PV	present value
PVI	present value index
PWI	present worth index
QALY	quality-adjusted life year
ROA	real options analysis
ROI	return on investment
RRR	required rate of return
SCC	social cost of carbon
SDG	sustainable development goals
SME	subject matter expert
SOC	social opportunity cost
SPC	shadow price of capital
SROI	social return on investment
SRTP	social rate of time preference
SWOT	strengths, weaknesses, opportunities, and threats

TBL	triple bottom line
TCO	total cost of ownership
TEMS	Technology and Engineering Management Society
UN	United Nations
USGBC	United States Green Building Council
VFM	value for money
VSL	value of a statistical life
STEER	socio-cultural, technological, economic, ecological, and regulatory
STEM	science, technology, engineering, and math
WACC	weighted average cost of capital
WCED	World Commission on Environment and Development
WTA	willingness to accept
WTP	willingness to pay

INTRODUCTION

Decision-making processes can be simple or complex, rigorous or messy, quantitative or qualitative (or both). They can be applied to the most mundane of actions (Should I have a peanut butter sandwich or a salad for lunch? Should I sleep in or get out of bed?) and can be scaled up to guide potential undertakings by major companies, nonprofit organizations, and governments. We make decisions every day, most of them undocumented. Our decisions are affected by our perspective, known and unknown biases, level of tolerance for risk, past experiences, amount of available information, access to funds/resources, deadlines, influence by others, and so much more. We don't always make the "right" decision, often discovering that after the fact.

The purpose of this book is to discuss the content and methodology of strategic project analysis, providing insight to traditional cost-benefit analysis, evaluation, operations research, and other business analytics and decision-making methods. The book opens by describing the traditional applications of economic analysis and evaluation in government and organizational decision-making. Concepts of stakeholders, risk, and project planning are introduced, followed by a brief overview of traditional quantitative concepts. The reader is then engaged with a more in-depth discourse about qualitative project elements, ethics, bias, and common challenges in project analysis. The author pivots to discuss major projects in the contexts of sustainability, resilience, failure, perspective, and non-traditional value. The book concludes with some thoughts on the future of strategic project analysis and the imperative to apply both qualitative and quantitative methods. Each chapter of the book includes problems, exercises, and opportunities for reflection.

DOI: 10.4324/9781003014928-1

WHAT MAKES THIS BOOK DIFFERENT?

This book delves into the shortcomings and common challenges in strategic project analysis, and advocates for a closer relationship between engineering economics and the practices of welfare economics and evaluation. Borrowing from both methodologies, the book discusses several specific scenarios for benefits identification using a multi-generational sustainable development viewpoint, uncovering hidden long-term sustainability and resilience benefits.

STRUCTURE OF THE BOOK

Before diving into the details of how to perform strategic project analysis, Chapter 1 discusses the two broad contexts in which it is used: engineering economics and welfare economics. Some background is provided, and concepts and basic calculations are described. This section includes examples of when (and by what type of entity) each methodology is typically used.

Chapter 2 explains the basic process for conducting analysis, using cost-benefit analysis as a starting point (although all analysis methods follow the same or a similar process). Each step is described in detail, and tools and guidelines are provided for improving analysis results and avoiding complications. Particular attention is paid to developing the analysis scope, the types of choices that need to be made during that step of the process, and the potential effects of those choices. Definitions of costs, benefits, and disbenefits are provided, with a list of examples. Approaches to (and issues with) quantification are then discussed, including costing, monetary values by proxy (shadow pricing), and the use of ordinal scales for ranking. Basic economic feasibility calculations are introduced next, followed by scenario ranking and selection. Concepts of assumptions and omissions are introduced and discussed. The section concludes with a discussion about benefits management and ex-post analysis.

Having introduced basic concepts and the analysis process, the book then proceeds to discuss specific elements of analysis in detail, by chapter. Chapter 3 introduces stakeholders, assurance, stakeholder engagement, and the concept of stakeholder standing as it applies to the analysis scope. Chapter 4 presents project risk identification, management, treatment, and inclusion in both financial analysis and evaluation.

At this point, the book begins to delve into greater detail on the specific methods of inquiry and calculations used in quantitative and qualitative analysis. Chapter 5 presents the primary calculations used in financial/economic analysis, with a discussion of how and why each is applied. Concepts such as schedule, cash flow, and interest and discount rates are introduced, as they relate to the calculations presented. The chapter concludes with a discussion about lifecycle cost analysis, as an example of cost-benefit analysis that is applied to the longest possible scenario duration. Chapter 6 then presents qualitative approaches to analysis that may be conducted in lieu of the quantitative approach or used to supplement quantitative analysis. The use, ease of application, and challenges of each approach are discussed, with some examples. The primary calculations used in evaluation are also presented, with a discussion of how each is applied. Concepts such as weighting, ordinal scales, and ranking are examined in more detail, adding to the information provided in Chapter 2. Finally, several blended approaches are introduced and discussed, which combine quantitative and qualitative methods.

Chapter 7 considers the effects that perspective, bias, and ethics have on the analysis. Different perspectives are described and discussed, and select biases are introduced, along with tips for overcoming those biases. The chapter concludes with a discussion about the ethical dimensions of each step in the analysis process.

Having provided the basics of both quantitative and qualitative analysis, the book then pivots to the perspective of the reader and recipient of a strategic project analysis report. Chapter 8 revisits the concepts introduced in Chapters 1–7, discussing them in the context of potential pitfalls in and obstacles to understanding the analysis report. Critical thinking is used to guide the reader to an understanding of report context and the effects that funding, perspective, and objective might have on the outcome of the analysis. Next, there is a discussion about report quality and contents. Finally, a list of questions is provided that can be used to guide the reader through the critical questioning process necessary to assure themselves of the rigor, transparency, and accuracy of the analysis, report, and scenario selection recommendations.

Chapter 9 introduces the concepts of sustainability and resilience in the context of societal value benefits and advocates for using sustainability and resilience goals to identify benefits and disbenefits during the analysis process. It discusses the timeframe required for benefits to be realized and the challenges that poses for analysis.

Finally, Chapter 10 considers strategic project analysis as applied for different types of projects, including the challenges experienced in analysis and the types of benefits that might be included or specifically excluded in the context of hidden long-term benefits and sustainability and resilience benefits.

Each chapter of the book includes questions designed for reflection, exercises, and problem sets as appropriate, and a reference list.

1

WHAT IS STRATEGIC PROJECT ANALYSIS?

Strategic project analysis is a mechanism for comparing several different scenarios designed to solve the same problem. It is a type of applied business research that utilizes systematic inquiry, rigorous research methods, and analytic skills. For the purposes of this discussion, benefits may be monetary gain (income or savings), opportunities, improvements, and/or other positive consequences that result from undertaking a scenario. Disbenefits are the flip side of benefits, negative consequences that result from undertaking a scenario. Costs are the monetary value of any resources utilized when implementing the scenario.

Let's start by introducing two schools of practice, which have similar objectives but different approaches, and are equally controversial.

Early articles and textbooks on engineering economics date back to at least the mid-1800s, likely even earlier. Basic concepts and calculations in cost-benefit analysis (CBA) are applied to evaluate the profitability of potential investment projects and choose between mutually exclusive alternatives, using calculations of economic benefit. The calculations focus on the cost of resources required to execute a project and the monetary value of benefits to be gained from the project, emphasizing optimization in resource use. In its simplest form, engineering economics is used in the manufacturing industry to analyze scenarios in which equipment needs to be replaced or augmented owing to age (end of useful life), or when an attractive technology advancement (upgrade) has become available. This is often applied in pharmaceutical and petrochemical projects, with both initial investment and operations and maintenance costs included in the analysis scope. On a larger

DOI: 10.4324/9781003014928-2

scale, these methods are employed (and sometimes required by funding source, company policy, or law) to evaluate entire major projects, as utilized in manufacturing, transportation, education, infrastructure, healthcare, software development, and major events. Strategic decision-making for major projects typically involves the commitment of significant resources and may critically impact the organizations involved by creating long-term consequences.

In parallel, welfare economics developed and evolved to evaluate the impact of programs and projects designed to solve specific societal problems and contribute to the "greater public good", embodying moral values through scenarios designed to result in a potential Pareto or Kaldor-Hicks improvement. In a Pareto scenario, the goal is to effect an improvement in a given situation that benefits one or more people without harming others; in reality, a true Pareto scenario is difficult to achieve. In a Kaldor-Hicks scenario, the analyst acknowledges benefits to one population and losses to another in a given scenario but is inclined to choose the scenario where the benefits exceed losses, enacting Thomas Aquinas's doctrine of double effect. It can be argued the Kaldor-Hicks criterion is more realistic and easier to achieve. When selecting between scenarios for a particular intervention, the state of the affected population is appraised both with and without the proposed intervention, measuring the anticipated incremental effect of the initiative on peoples' lives. The approach is typically microeconomic, focusing on the behavior of persons (individuals and companies) related to the allocation of resources. These methods are also used to choose between investments in different societal initiatives given a limited set of funds (constrained project selection) and develop evidence-based government policies. The analysis may include the alternative or option of taking no action. Benefit-cost analysis (BCA, note the difference in terminology compared with economic analysis CBA) and cost-effectiveness analysis are applied by governments around the world, intergovernmental organizations such as the United Nations (UN), related agencies (such as the World Health Organization, UNICEF, and UNESCO), and non-governmental organizations such as the International Red Cross. From here forward in this book, welfare economics practice is referred to as evaluation.

REFLECTIONS

1. What are some major differences between engineering economics and welfare economics?
2. Name five (5) entities (not already named) that might utilize engineering economics methods. Explain why.
3. Name five (5) entities (not already named) that might utilize welfare economics methods. Explain why.
4. What type of investments might necessitate engineering economics analysis? Name five (5) and explain why.
5. What type of investments might entail welfare economics analysis? Name five (5) and explain why.
6. In your own words, explain the difference between a Pareto scenario and a Kaldor-Hicks scenario.
7. When you make decisions, are they typically based on cost and/or profit, soft benefits, or a combination thereof? Explain and provide two (2) examples.

BIBLIOGRAPHY

Aquinas, T. (13th c.), reprint by The Aquinas Institute (2012). *Summa Theologiae*. Steubenville: St. Paul Center for Biblical Theology.

Hicks, J. (1939). *The Foundations of Welfare Economics. The Economic Journal*, 49(196): 696–712.

Kaldor, N. (1939). *Welfare Propositions in Economics and Interpersonal Comparisons of Utility. The Economic Journal*, 49(195): 549–552.

Pareto, V. (1896–97). *Cours d'Économie Politique*. Lausanne: F. Rouge.

Yates, B.T. and Marra, M. (2017). *Introduction: Social Return on Investment (SROI)*. Evaluation and Program Planning, 64, 95–97.

2

ANALYSIS PLANNING

In both engineering economics and evaluation, choosing a scenario utilizes both decision-making tools and project-planning processes. Planning, for the purposes of analysis, can be divided into five phases that follow a process of classical rational decision-making and management:

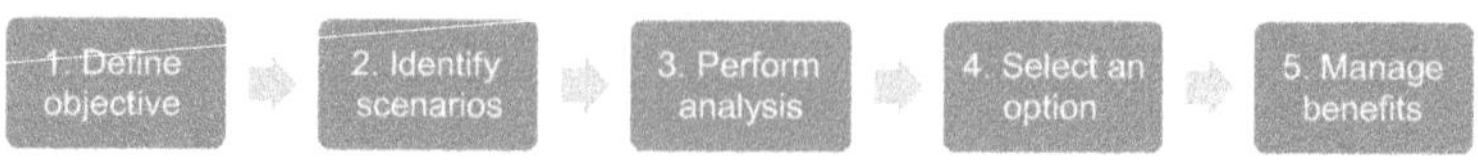

Figure 2.1 Decision-making process

While these simplified steps are represented here as linear (sequential), the process is often iterative with a loop from step 4 back to step 3 or step 2 as appropriate. From here forward in the book, please read "scenario" as either "project" or "initiative" as it suits your situation, organization, or industry.

DEFINING THE OBJECTIVE

The first phase in the analysis process is to define the project objective. Defining the objective is not the same as defining scope; it is actually a predecessor to scope and scenario development, which occur in phase two of the process (as shown in Figure 2.1). The project objective can be described as the desired outcome of the project. Keep it simple and at a fairly high level – the next phase is where complexity can be added.

Defining an objective may be as straightforward as having already identified a problem and having a desire to solve that problem. In

DOI: 10.4324/9781003014928-3

such an instance, the undesirable elements of the situation can be listed, along with their opposites. For example, if your washing machine has stopped working, the basic objective would be to have a washing machine that works properly[1]. Deciding whether to repair it or purchase a new one comes later.

However, it might not be that easy. An objective may defined in the context of performance, business strategy, financial goals, economic competition, process or quality improvement and optimization, external regulation, cultural or societal situation, technology change, and more. It may be broad or very specific, long-term or short-term, resulting in a deliverable output or outcome, or even multiple outcomes. Defining an objective often requires soliciting stakeholder input (see Chapter 3 of this book), which may necessitate collaboration in the form of a team workshop or public outreach.

An objective must be clear and concise, reference the needs assessment, and be measurable - this becomes important both during the project and for retrospective analytics. The SMART system (developed in 1981 by George Doran et al.) is a good framework for this exercise. The SMART process requires goals to be Specific, Measurable, Attainable, Relevant, and Time-Limited. Another approach would be to adapt value management methods, stating the objective as simply as possible. Functional analysis, a tool used in traditional value engineering, requires stating an item's function using only a verb-noun combination[2] (in the case of the washing machine, the purpose of the machine would be to cleanse fabrics). Ultimately, the project objective is written as a self-contained statement.

During this phase, it is appropriate to document a description of the situation and context, current performance or issues, and any other information that may be useful in developing plans to achieve the stated objective and deciding on the breadth (scope) of the analysis. Documentation should also be kept from workshops and meetings.

IDENTIFYING SCENARIOS

Next, the objective statement is used to identify potential commensurable solutions to the problem and/or approaches to achieving the stated objective. These potential solutions are known as "alternatives" or "scenarios", each of which meets the stated objectives and requirements to some degree. Scenarios are identified through business intelligence and forecasting. Business intelligence uses past and current data to guide business decisions and strategy by gaining insights, drawing conclusions, and identifying potential recourse. Forecasting imagines the future state of the organization.

Quantitative analysis readily lends itself to comparing scenarios designed to achieve the same objective. However, strategic project analysis is sometimes used to consider a wishlist of projects that have different objectives. This is typically done in a corporation or government setting where different departments or agencies are competing for funding within a fixed budget pool. For such a situation, qualitative methods are flexible by design.

Every analysis must include the consideration of at least two realistic and viable scenarios (analysis of alternatives) and may include the option of taking no action (maintaining the status quo), thus contemplating a counterfactual baseline scenario. It might not be possible to consider the "do nothing" scenario, in which case it is reasonable to consider "do minimum" as an option. Typical cost-benefit analyses limit the number of scenarios to a maximum of four. There is a certain psychological strategy involved in choosing to evaluate four scenarios. It prevents the selection of the middle or most moderate alternative and forces deeper inspection. Narrowing the population of scenarios to four may require qualitative ranking and/or preliminary quantitative analysis and elimination of scenarios as discussed in Chapters Five (quantitative calculations) and Six (qualitative analysis) of this book.

The identification and subsequent development of scenarios will require both broad brainstorming and specific input from both project designers and stakeholders – this is no small task. The scenario development process may involve demand analysis or projections, identification of requirements, a resource management plan, identification of weaknesses, feasibility study, identification of funding sources, and the drafting of a preliminary schedule (timeline) for project completion. Independent experts and specialists may be consulted. This collection of data will also be used during the next phase, analysis. Scenario development may utilize skills found in scenario planning and systems thinking, as applied to inputs and outputs, positive and negative effects, relationships, external forces, and patterns of behavior.

It is generally understood that scenario development will be conducted at a preliminary or basic level owing to both a lack of available information and reluctance to invest in detailed development, design, and engineering until the population of scenarios is further reduced through analysis. Scenarios must be right-sized, which can be achieved by managing requirements. The MoSCoW prioritization method can be used to identify must-haves, should-haves, could-haves, and wish-to-haves, narrowing the scenarios to their most important and/or non-negotiable elements. As a rule, just enough definition is required to be able to meaningfully distinguish between the different scenarios during the analysis phase. Any exclusions must be documented and clearly stated in the analysis report. Returning to the washing machine example, scenarios might include replacing the washing machine with a comparable machine, upgrading to a more sophisticated machine, repairing it, or doing nothing. After the first round of analysis has been conducted, scenarios may be developed in more detail and re-analyzed using the new data.

Analysis scope

Identifying scenarios also necessitates understanding the scope of the analysis to be performed. Defining scope often means delimiting the analysis and establishing boundaries for the theoretical exercise as deemed necessary, usually owing to resource constraints. In theory, the economic analysis of a scenario should be all-inclusive (synoptic), evaluating all known costs and benefits. In reality, this is not practical, and analysis may be typically limited to potentially significant impacts and decision-relevant aspects (see: sensitivity test in Chapter 4 of this book) lest the sheer volume of data become unwieldy. Traditional cost-benefit analyses are necessarily reductionist, not least because the analysis itself can be very expensive and time-consuming to perform. When establishing the analysis scope, the breadth and depth of analysis should be appropriate for its decision-making purpose. Scope definition should be practical, just thorough enough for the analyst to reach a justifiable and well-reasoned conclusion without oversimplifying. If at all possible, the budget allocated for the analysis should be sufficient enough to prevent any detrimental restriction of scope and methodology.

In the context of time (the planning horizon), the analysis scope may include the project phases of development and implementation and may extend to analysis of the first few years of operation, the time horizon required to measure the economic impact of the scenario, or even the full duration of the organization's need. In the context of machinery, the useful life of the equipment will determine the planning horizon. Useful life is the number of years an item can be reasonably expected to serve reliably and at capacity before it needs to be overhauled or replaced. It is less common for the planning horizon limit to include multiple generations or be set to infinity, except where benefits take decades (such as in science and research investments, and transport) or even hundreds of years (such as with certain policy interventions) to materialize.

Similarly, the impact area (territory affected by the proposed project) used for analysis is rarely comprehensive. Stakeholder analysis (discussed in Chapter 3 of this book) can be used to identify beneficiaries and negatively affected populations within the impact area, further defining and limiting the analysis scope to those with demonstrated standing.

Certain elements of the project (such as risks, intangibles, or opportunity costs) may be excluded from the analysis, owing to the time and resources required to analyze those elements or limitations created by the lack of available data (bounded rationality). Opportunity costs (or economic costs) are the effects of the missed opportunity created by choosing one scenario over another, such as benefits, revenue, and costs foregone when the next-best scenario is not chosen. Third-party costs and benefits and pecuniary or secondary effects (such as changes in income distribution or supply and demand) may also be ignored, depending on the perspective of the analysis.

There will be a diminishing rate of return on the analysis process at a certain level of detail or granularity, such that it might not be worth expending effort on project elements that rank low in priority or the sensitivity analysis. Few cost-benefit analyses are truly comprehensive. Any omissions and ground rules and assumptions must be documented and clearly stated in the analysis report.

PERFORMING ANALYSIS

Having identified a handful of scenarios, the next phase of the process is to conduct analysis. There are many different approaches available, depending upon the characteristics of the scenario(s), available data, level of complexity, and level of effort to be invested in the examination. A simple economic approach is described here, with more detailed methodologies described in Chapter 5 (Quantitative calculations) and 6 (Qualitative analysis) of this book.

Identifying costs, benefits, and disbenefits

The simplest way to keep track of costs and benefits is to create a list. Identifying and predicting realistic costs and benefits will require brainstorming and input from stakeholders, who will contribute their specific knowledge and experience. It is not unusual for organizations to look to similar past projects to identify line items; however, no two projects are exactly alike and some insight will always be necessary regarding any differences.

When brainstorming, it may help first to categorize elements of the project by system and identify line items within each system, circling back later to consider the project as a whole. Any resulting economic disadvantages or undesirable outcomes, known as disbenefits, are also identified. Benefits and disbenefits may result from market, institutional, or behavioral distortions owing to the implementation of a scenario.

Readily quantifiable costs for a project may include (but might not be limited to):

- Labor resources (internal)
- Consultants (external)
- Equipment purchase or rental
- Materials
- Software purchase or license subscription
- Subcontracted services (external)
- Utilities
- Building rent
- Land purchase
- Transportation and travel costs
- Revenue
- Taxes and fees
- Financing costs
- Start-up costs

- Operating costs, including maintenance and administration
- Residual values of assets
- Administrative costs and savings
- Regulatory compliance costs
- Decommissioning
- Donated materials and services

In its purest form, a cost-benefit analysis will quantify every possible use of resources and every possible source of revenue. For practical reasons, this is rarely done. However, it is a worthwhile exercise to identify as many potential cost and revenue line items as possible, and then decide and document which to include or omit. If there are sunk costs (money that has already been spent) or planned expenditures that are the same across all scenarios, they can be documented and then ignored for analysis because only the cost and benefit differences between scenarios are considered.

STEER is a framework used in business analysis (BA) for identifying influences related to the external macro environment. The acronym stands for socio-cultural, technological, economic, ecological, and regulatory factors, and is similar to PEST, PESTEL, ETPS, and other BA frameworks. In this context, it can be used to identify costs and benefits related to external factors. The STEER framework is not dissimilar to the risk categories described in Chapter 4 of this book.

Whereas direct costs are fairly straightforward to identify, benefits and disbenefits may be more difficult to isolate owing to the challenges of understanding and justifying cause and effect. Outcomes from a scenario (intervention) must be realistically linked to actions taken within the scenario, and any correlation well described. Issues of intersectionality, indirect and third-party effects, and apophenia (incorrectly perceived correlation) are particularly difficult to identify, isolate, quantify, and analyze.

The following is a short list of qualitative (nonmarket) project outcomes:

- Improved compliance
- Reduced pollution
- Reduced traffic
- Fewer accidents (safety)

- Shorter travel time (convenience)
- Improved physical and mental health
- Better quality of life
- Job creation
- Staff retention
- Reduced workload
- Productivity increase
- Innovation and creativity
- Net zero carbon emission targets
- Preservation of species
- Human dignity
- Reduced crime
- Upskilling
- Accessibility

These, and other benefits, are described in more detail in Chapter 9 of this book. Note that each of these is stated as a benefit; each could also be stated as a disbenefit, or as a risk effect. Each of the items listed above and in Chapter 9 of this book could warrant an entire study unto itself, which is unlikely to happen just for one analysis owing to resource (time and cost) constraints. However, a study might be exactly what is needed to quantify and monetize the outcome for future analyses and industry or discipline knowledge. Relationships between outcomes, where there are multiple outcomes from a scenario, may be described using regression analysis.

Once identified, items should be grouped into categories as appropriate; doing so will help identify any duplication (double-counting), gaps, and overlap. A scenario may have more than one objective, when it is designed to generate an array of planned benefits; for such scenarios, line items may be grouped by objective. Purely economic analyses tend to divide line items into four nominal categories (direct, indirect, overhead, and intangible), and will also identify the year (or month, depending on the project time scale) in which the expenditure or revenue is expected to be realized. Many intangibles require a long timeframe before they can occur and be measured. This cash flow timing (discussed in Chapter 5 of this book) will be necessary later in the analysis when performing cost-benefit calculations for short- and long-term line items. For reasons that will be explained below, benefits should also be prioritized according to desirability and materiality.

Quantifying costs and benefits

The next step in the process is to select an appropriate appraisal methodology. For the purposes of this chapter, it is assumed a traditional purely quantitative (economic) cost-benefit analysis is being conducted. Other approaches are discussed in Chapters Five (quantitative calculations) and Six (qualitative analysis) of this book.

Quantification utilizes skills found in estimating and valuation. Please see the end of this chapter for estimating resources. There are many types of value, such as fair market value (price), replacement value, esteem value, liquidation value, and salvage value. Use value and non-use value may also be relevant. For the purposes of strategic project analysis, if a resource can be used or valued in several different ways, its value should be calculated as if applied in its best (or most beneficial) use. This type of value is known as opportunity value.

As with identifying costs and benefits, it is not unusual for organizations to look to similar past projects, utilizing reference class forecasting and extrapolating from historical data to both quantify and value potential costs and benefits. Information used for analysis may be scientific, technical, or economic. The team may engage assistance and obtain primary data from data records, accounting, asset management, contracts, and procurement departments. For unique projects and resources, specialized knowledge may come from subject matter experts and/or other consultants. Additional information may be obtained from external sources, and secondary data may be obtained through interviews, surveys, focus groups, and expert panels.

The achievable level of accuracy and reliability for both quantities and pricing depends on the amount of data available at the time of analysis, the current level of detail in scenario definition and design, the uniqueness of the scenario, and the existence of a competitive market for the goods and services being valued. No valuation is perfectly accurate; all quantities and costing contain limitations and some degree of error and uncertainty, which should be documented to avoid creating a false sense of precision.

In order to ensure consistency in analysis and a commensurable "apples-to-apples" comparison, costs and benefits must be valued in the same units – cost-benefit analysis and other quantitative methods are usually a mono-criterion method of analysis. Costs and benefits are usually stated in monetary present-day amounts; future costs are addressed in other calculations, discussed in Chapter 5 of this book. Although any estimates will, by their very nature, become out of date almost immediately, it is important to remember that analysis results are most influenced by magnitude and thus unaffected by minor imprecision.

Nonmarket benefits and disbenefits may be assigned a monetary value by proxy, using shadow pricing. For example, accidents and improved health may be measured in terms of value per life (value of a statistical life), or the cost of medical services or restitution. Pollution and compliance may be measurable in the context of penalties paid, extended infrastructure life, difference in fuel required, marginal abatement cost, or the social cost of carbon. Other line items may be estimated using an individual's willingness to pay (WTP) to obtain the beneficial outcome or, conversely, willingness to accept (WTA) compensation in the absence of said outcome.

Shadow pricing methods for non-market outputs typically require undertaking a study of the benefit or disbenefit and include (but are not limited to):

- Contingent valuation captures individuals' stated preferences using interviews or surveys.
- Revealed preferences uses historic data from individuals' behavior to assign values.
- Hedonic pricing applies a mathematical model to analyze both internal and external characteristics and factors on individuals' revealed preferences. It is often used for housing prices.
- Travel cost may be used to assign value to recreational activities and environmental amenities.

These are, at best, subjective approximations of non-market outputs which may be based on feelings and opinions. Value assignments are often controversial, alongside concerns that they are incommensurable with market values and reduce multi-dimensional problems to uni-dimensional. There are many approaches to the measurement and quantification of societal impacts, with little consistency across the methodologies. Whenever weighting and alternate valuation methods are applied, there should be narrative support and source documentation should be maintained to justify the weighting and the assignment of value.

It is also worth noting that, by allocating a weighted or unweighted hypothetical economic amount to a qualitative element, a misleading sense of relative value and equivalence might be created. For example, $1 million in revenue is not necessarily the same as a life valued at $1 million; the two are not interchangeable.

There are many methods available for quantifying non-financial benefits and disbenefits, with much inconsistency across them. Some specialized software packages are also available, and published monetization exists from previous studies. However, every monetization is specific to the stakeholder group surveyed and outcomes measured from the project for which it was developed. The monetization might not be appropriate if applied to a different project. When using commercial software or monetization from a pre-existing study, the study/software objectives, funding source, stakeholders, date (age), and more should be well understood and documented, and the analyst must confirm the data is suitable for the purposes of the new analysis.

Where monetary value cannot be assigned or used as a proxy, such as for intangible benefits and disbenefits, a numeric (ordinal) scale may be used to assign an objective relative score with a narrative provided to describe relevant effects. Examples of such intangibles include reputation, brand awareness, aesthetics, morale, customer satisfaction, and knowledge improvement. The Likert scale is the most common ordinal scale, with a scoring range of one through 5, 7, 9, or 11 (always an odd number). For example, a well-being analysis may value outcomes in well-being units. An approach that utilizes a combination of methods that lack a common denominator is called a multi-criteria method; multi-criteria approaches are discussed in Chapter 6 of this book.

It is highly likely that monetary direct (and some indirect) costs will be fairly easy to identify and calculate but some (if not many) benefits and disbenefits will be impossible to quantify and monetize owing to lack of data, modeling difficulties, incommensurability, cost of analysis, lack of time or resources, and more. Unquantified benefits and disbenefits are a systemic, pervasive, and unsolved problem in cost-benefit analysis. Excluding benefits means the benefits side of the equation will be undercounted and the relative magnitude of benefits will be understated, preventing meaningful analysis and skewing any results. As mentioned above, benefits should always be prioritized. If a significant number of high-priority and important benefits cannot be quantified, a legitimate quantitative analysis cannot be performed and a qualitative approach to strategic project analysis becomes necessary, utilizing a method that maximizes net benefits.

Scenario scope and pricing are subject to errors in forecasting and prediction, and may be affected by changes in the schedule, future regulatory requirements, and leaps in technology. It is the nature of strategic project analysis for more data to become available as the analysis progresses, owing either to newly identified sources or more mature project definitions. If enough new information is obtained and/or changes in estimated values become significant, the team may consider re-doing the analysis.

Quantification is affected by the analysis scope definition. Many publicly funded scenario analyses are restricted to a particular timeframe (such as initial investment), to ensure expenditures will fit within a pre-determined budgetary range. Private sector scenarios, in contrast, usually focus on minimizing total lifecycle cost, conducting a full lifecycle cost estimate that includes operating expenditures and costs or benefits at project termination (such as salvage value). When comparing full lifecycle costs for several scenarios, the outcome may differ from a simple comparison of the initial investments (first cost), owing to costs incurred such as scheduled and unscheduled maintenance, materials and parts inventory, overhead, risk, equipment replacement or overhaul, and more.

When performing quantification, it is appropriate to document all assumptions and omissions, and note whether the amounts stated are from vendor quotations, publicly listed pricing, alternate methods, study, or an estimate. Justification for the use of WTP vs WTA (or vice versa) should be provided. Supporting documentation for all costing and preliminary schedules should be retained and dated. It may be helpful to assign the estimates a degree of confidence, using a five point Likert scale.

Economic feasibility

Net benefits are the sum of benefits (positive) and disbenefits (negative).

$$Net\ Benefits = Benefits - Disbenefits$$

Equation 2.1 Net benefits

For the very simplest of project cost-benefit analysis calculations, where all benefits and costs are stated in present value and there are no qualitatively scored elements considered, total costs (C) can be subtracted from net benefits (B) to determine economic feasibility.

$$Economic\ Feasibility = Net\ Benefits - Costs$$

Equation 2.2 Economic feasibility

For a project to be considered economically feasible, the total project benefits (expected to be) received should exceed the total resources to be invested – in other words, $B-C > 0$.

Note that evaluation methods may choose to omit the time value of money and may use total benefits in calculations instead of net benefits. Variations of this sort in calculations can yield very different results and thus can influence the selection of scenarios; as such, the selection and use of equations may surface bias and ethical issues. Economic feasibility and return on investment calculations are particularly affected by such variations. If simplification of equations is preferred, the analyst should perform both the original and simplified calculations, and then compare them as a sensitivity test, discussed next. There is more discussion on this topic in Chapter 5 of this book.

Return on investment

Return on investment (ROI) is a measurement of economic attractiveness and profitability, calculated as the ratio of net tangible financial gains (profit or change in value) to investment cost. It is one of the two most common calculations in financial analysis, the other being Net Present Value (NPV), discussed in Chapter 5 of this book. Another way of expressing the equation is:

$$ROI = \frac{Net\ Economic\ Benefit}{Investment\ Cost}$$

Equation 2.3 Return on investment

ROI is always stated as a percentage and may be calculated per year. ROI is a simple calculation that can be applied in advance of a more comprehensive analysis. A positive ROI is preferred (in other words, $B/C > 0$); if ROI is negative, it means no profit will be made.

In evaluation practice, the ROI computation may be performed without first stating all variables as present values (see the time value of money, discussed in Chapter 5 of this book), but that approach will yield a very approximate and thus less accurate result. Purely financial/economic analysis applies present values, considering the time value of money in the calculation.

An alternate approach, known as Discounted ROI, uses in the equation the net present value of benefits and costs. Another common financial analysis calculation is Implicit ROI, which is the ROI at which $NPV = 0$. Implicit ROI will always be lower than ROI (Implicit ROI < ROI). More detailed discussion of cost-benefit analysis calculations can be found in Chapter 5 of this book.

Sensitivity test

Sensitivity testing, or what-if simulation, can help inform the strategic project analysis by identifying how changes to specific independent line items, assumptions, equations, and criteria affect the results. Items that have a significant impact are known as critical variables. A sensitivity test is a deterministic form of risk analysis conducted by varying individual line-item values and other parameters or assumptions (such as cash flow timing) to see what effect each change has on the quantitative analysis output. Understanding the scenario's sensitivity to changes and uncertainty in certain variables helps the analyst fine-tune weighting and scoring, optimize resource allocation, and correct errors. The less sensitivity there is in the model, the more robust the analysis.

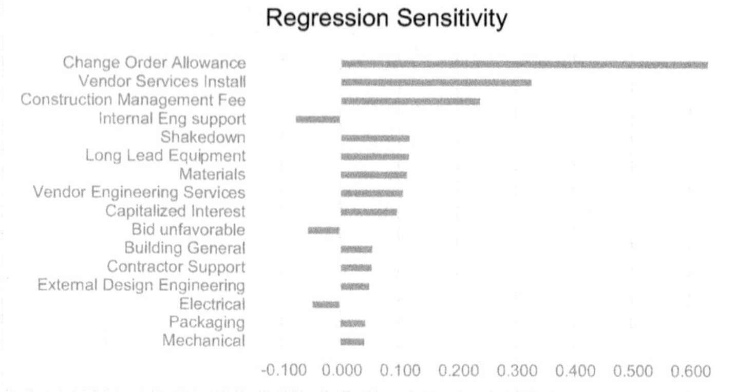

Figure 2.2 Tornado diagram[3]

Sensitivity testing may be done incrementally, performing a small handful of re-calculations by modifying a single variable such as interest rate; this is called local, univariate, or partial sensitivity analysis. Sensitivity testing may also be done using statistical modeling software to simulate the effects of modifications to multiple variables; this is called global or multivariate sensitivity analysis. The use of Monte Carlo simulation software enables the analyst to test thousands of random changes.

Sensitivity results are typically graphed for easier comprehension of relative impact. Sensitivity may be depicted as a tornado diagram, a horizontal bar chart that depicts potential variability, ranking variables from highest to lowest based on their level of influence.

The tornado diagram above illustrates the relative impacts on the analysis outcome associated with cost line items for a construction project.

SELECTING AN OPTION

Scenario ranking

The last step in the analysis is to rank the scenarios. In this process, the scenarios are listed in order, from most to least desirable. It is expected that all ranked scenarios will meet a minimum threshold of acceptability, as defined by scoring criteria. In the case of revenue-generating projects, the ranking will likely be in declining order of projected revenue, representing the relative measurement of ophelimity (economic usefulness). If a maximum cost (investment) threshold has been established, scenarios may be eliminated if their cost exceeds the constraint. Similarly, scenarios may be eliminated if their projected revenue does not reach a pre-established minimum threshold.

When viewed from a purely economic stance, it is probable that the highest-ranking scenario will be the option selected, barring other informational inputs. However, the determination of the "best" alternative may be influenced by subjective elements and consider input from other decision-making processes, incentives, and analyses, resulting in a high-ranking scenario that is different from that generated by purely economic measures.

Iterative process

As mentioned previously, the process steps listed above may be iterative. The first pass of analysis may be less detailed for screening purposes, intended to identify fatal flaws and reduce the population of alternative scenarios by eliminating those least economically feasible. If so, the team will then return to scenario development and analysis at a more detailed level for the finalist alternatives, especially if the technical design has progressed in a parallel effort and more data has become available. A more comprehensive analysis may also be conducted to best understand the selected option.

Report

The report is both a means of communication and an artifact of project governance – it provides information to decision-makers and stakeholders, bringing attention to the conclusions reached through analysis while also serving as a permanent record of the effort. Governance is the set of policies, procedures, and processes that guide organizational decision-making and management accountability. The report itself needs to be specifically written for its audience, using appropriate language and level of detail. It should be concise while at the same time including all necessary information for decision-making and excluding irrelevant material. An executive summary should appear early in the report, in which the analysis conclusions and key information are condensed. The body of the report then provides more detail about the analysis process, data, assumptions, and results, with clear justification of the conclusion. The report should also include narrative describing how qualitative data impacts the scenarios, the results from the sensitivity test, and any implications owing to analysis limitations. Most important of all, the report needs to be timely; good information received too late serves no purpose.

Documentation and records

Once analysis is complete, and an option selected, it is time to review and cross-check all documentation to ensure it is complete. The analysis process and project selection justification should be well documented and kept as part of project records. It is considered best practice to collect documentation throughout the analysis process, from day one. Appropriate annotation and coding may be used to ease future review and audit.

Calculations should be able to be replicated, selection of analysis method explained, funding source identified, all assumptions and obstacles documented, omissions and exclusions (such as sunk costs) listed, sensitivity test results described, and the analysis process itself presented so as to be credible with sound reasoning. All data sources, data collection methods, and documentation used in the analysis should be cited and the analysis team identified, including both internal staff and external consultants. Lack of documentation is an indicator the analysis and investment decision-making processes may have been compromised or lacked quality control.

BENEFITS MANAGEMENT

Benefits may begin to appear while the project is being implemented and will continue to manifest over its lifetime. Both value creation and destruction from the project should be measured periodically, and managed throughout the project. This can be achieved through a structured benefits management process.

Benefits and potential disbenefits can be identified, categorized, and described using information from the strategic project analysis process, and realistic target values established against which progress (benefits achievement) can be measured. Target values may be obtained from past projects, or benchmarked against similar organizations. These are the criteria for project success. Some outcomes (and related benefits/disbenefits) might not be directly measurable, in which case narrative accounts or a scoring mechanism may be required for progress reporting.

A regular cadence for data capture, monitoring, and reporting should be established, and specific and consistent data-gathering methods established. The process is cyclical and very similar to the one for risk management discussed in Chapter 4 of this book. A chain of project documentation is necessary for the performance of benefits management. To that end, data and documentation must be collected and archived from the proposing organization, funding entity, developer/builder, owner, and operator. This document management and data collection process should be established early in the project as part of the standardized policies and procedures and governance, and funding allocated for the effort as part of the project budget.

It is likely that additional, unexpected (emergent) benefits and disbenefits will also appear during the course of the project. These can be added to the list, and quantified and reported accordingly.

EX-POST ANALYSIS

A retrospective (ex-post) analysis can be performed to understand the actual benefits and costs of a project or initiative, especially for public sector projects, social welfare initiatives, and policymaking. Strategic project analysis is not a controlled experiment; it has many moving parts and factors that sometimes cannot be identified in advance. As such, a retrospective analysis is very useful. There is a chance that, because the ex-post analysis uses actual data, the analysis will be less biased than an ex-ante analysis but may include hindsight bias. The analysis may take the form of a project performance assessment report, an audit, or may simply be an update to or expansion of a previous analysis. Ex-post analysis also considers a counter-factual scenario in which the project was never built (the do-nothing scenario) or a do-minimum scenario, against which to compare the current situation.

An ex-post analysis may be required by the project funding source (the World Bank and others), or may be required by law (Europe, United Kingdom). In evaluation practice, where qualitative methods may have been used to justify a project and approval to proceed has already been received, an analysis may be performed ex-post facto (after the fact) to further justify the expenditure (in which case strategic misrepresentation may be incentivized to ensure consistency with the initial recommendation).

Any ex-post analysis should use the same metrics/measurable objectives as defined during step one of the original analysis process. Conducting this analysis (also called a validation exercise) provides the opportunity to measure what has actually happened, allowing valuable insight to whether the scenario was implemented as planned, and target costs and benefits incurred and achieved as expected. Additional cause-and-effect relationships may be identified, along with unexpected (fortuitous) benefits. The analysis also contributes to historical data and lessons learned, and the data obtained may be used for modeling future analyses.

A chain of project documentation is necessary for the performance of ex-post analysis. To that end, data and documentation must be collected and archived from the proposing organization, funding entity, developer/builder, owner, and operator. This document management and data collection process should be established early in the project as part of the standardized policies and procedures and governance, and funding allocated for the effort as part of the project budget.

PROBLEMS AND REFLECTIONS

1. See Figure 2.1. Why might the analysis revert to step three? Explain.
2. See Figure 2.1. Why might the analysis revert to step two? Explain.
3. What is the difference between "do nothing" and "do minimum"? Explain in your own words.
4. Explain why no two projects can ever be exactly the same. Provide an example.
5. Consider a scenario in which you are purchasing tickets to a concert. What might be your WTP for each ticket? Consider a

scenario in which you own the concert tickets and the concert is sold out. What might be your WTA to give up the tickets? Discuss the difference between your WTP and WTA for this scenario.

6. Benefits are $10,000 and costs are $8,500. Demonstrate whether or not the project is economically feasible by using two different methods of calculation.
7. Benefits are $105,000, disbenefits are $25,000, and costs are $80,500. Demonstrate whether or not the project is economically feasible by using two different methods of calculation.
8. Discuss how you might identify potential costs, benefits, and disbenefits for a major sporting event such as the FIFA World Cup. Name at least five (5) and explain.
9. Why is analysis documentation important? Name at least five (5) ways it might be used in the future and explain.
10. Name ten (10) types of documentation that might be created or obtained during an analysis.

NOTES

1 The author really did purchase a new washing machine while writing this book.

2 This is more difficult to do than it first appears owing to issues of specificity. In the washing machine example, the author first wrote "clean clothes" and then realized the typical machine is used for more than just clothes, necessitating deeper analysis. The common denominator for clothes, shoes, sheets, and towels is fabric.

3 Nalewaik, A. (2020). *Project Cost Recording and Reporting*, p. 85. Abingdon: Routledge.

BIBLIOGRAPHY

APM. *What is Benefits Management and Project Success?* Retrieved on March 27, 2024 from www.apm.org.uk/resources/what-is-project-management/what-is-benefits-management-and-project-success.

Breese, R., Jenner, S., Serra, C., and Thorp, J. (2015). Benefits Management: Lost or Found in Translation. *International Journal of Project Management*, 33(7): 1438–1451.

Campen, James T. (1986). *Benefit, Cost, and Beyond: The Political Economy of Benefit-Cost Analysis*. Cambridge, MA: Ballinger.

Doran, G.T. (1981). There's a SMART Way to Write Management's Goals and Objectives. *Journal of Management Review*, 70: 35–36.

Florio, M. and Vignetti, S. (2013). *The Use of Ex Post Cost-Benefit Analysis to Assess the Long-Term Effects of Major Infrastructure Projects*. Centre for Industrial Studies, Working Paper N, 02/2013.

Flyvbjerg, B., and Bester, D.W. (2021). The Cost-Benefit Fallacy: Why Cost-Benefit Analysis Is Broken and How to Fix It. *Journal of Benefit-Cost Analysis*, October 2021, 1–25.

Government Accountability Office (2018). *Assessment Methodology for Economic Analysis.* GAO-18–151SP. Washington, DC: United States Government Accountability Office.

Government Accountability Office (2020). *GAO Cost Estimating and Assessment Guide.* GAO-20–195G. Washington, DC: United States Government Accountability Office.

Herman, P.M., Avery, D.J., Schemp, C.S., and Walsh, M.E. (2009). Are Cost-Inclusive Evaluations Worth the Effort? *Evaluation and Program Planning*, 32: 55–61.

Green, S. and Sergeeva, N. (2019). Value Creation in Projects: Towards a Narrative Perspective. *International Journal of Project Management*, 37(5): 636–651.

IEEE (2023). *IEEE Technology and Engineering Management Society Body of Knowledge (TEMSBOK)*. Hoboken, NJ: Wiley-IEEE Press.

IEG (2010). *Cost-Benefit Analysis in World Bank Projects*. Washington, DC: The International Bank for Reconstruction and Development/The World Bank.

Lock, D. (Ed.) (2021). *The Practitioner Handbook of Project Controls*. Abingdon: Routledge.

Musawir, A., Serra, C., Zwikael, O., and Ali, I. (2017). Project Governance, Benefit Management, and Project Success: Towards a Framework for Supporting Organizational Strategy Implementation. *International Journal of Project Management*, 35(8): 1658–1672.

Nalewaik, A. (2020). *Project Cost Recording and Reporting*. Abingdon: Routledge.

Nicolaisen, M.S. and Driscoll, P.A. (2016). An International Review of Ex-Post Evaluation Schemes in the Transport Sector. *Journal of Environmental Assessment Policy and Management* (10)1: 1–33.

Office of Management and Budget (November 9, 2023). *Circular No. A-4, Regulatory Analysis*. Washington, DC: Executive Office of the President.

PMI (2020). *Practice Standard for Estimating, Second Edition*. Newtown Square: Project Management Institute.

PMI (2021). *A Guide to the Project Management Body of Knowledge (PMBOK), Seventh Edition*. Newtown Square: Project Management Institute.

RS Means (2009). *Estimating Handbook, Third Edition*. Greenville, SC: Gordian.

Sunstein, C. (2000). Cognition and Cost-Benefit Analysis. *The Journal of Legal Studies*, 29(S2): 1059–1103.

The White House (1993). Executive Order 12866: Regulatory Planning and Review. *Federal Register*, 58(190).

United States Environmental Protection Agency (2000). *Guidelines for Preparing Economic Analysis*. Washington, DC: Office of the Administrator.

United States Office of Management and Budget (January 11, 1996). *Economic Analysis of Federal Regulations Under Executive Order 12866*. Washington, DC: Executive Office of the President.

Yates, B.T. (1985). Cost-Effectiveness Analysis and Cost-Benefit Analysis: An Introduction. *Behavioral Assessment,* 7: 207–234.

Yates, B.T. (2021). Toward Collaborative Cost-Inclusive Evaluation: Adaptations and Transformations for Evaluators and Economists. *Evaluation and Program Planning*, 89.

Yates, B.T. and Persaud, N. (2023). *Cost-Inclusive Evaluation: Planning It, Doing It, Using It*. New York: The Guilford Press.

Zwikael, O. (2024). Benefits Classification to Enhance Project Value Creation. *International Journal of Project Management,* 42(2).

Zwikael, O., Chih, Y., and Meredith, J. (2018). Project Benefit Management: Setting Effective Target Benefits. *International Journal of Project Management,* 36(4): 650–658.

Zwikael, O. and Huemann, M. (2023). Project Benefits Management: Making an Impact on Organizations and Society Through Projects and Programs. *International Journal of Project Management,* 41(8).

3

STAKEHOLDERS

As discussed in the process phases one through three, an understanding of and interaction with stakeholders is integral to cost-benefit analysis. Although traditional economic analysis is primarily a tool used by management and finance, certain internal and external stakeholders also control information that is needed during the analysis. Further, stakeholder priorities may influence weighting, and stakeholder values and perspectives on success may influence the outcome of the analysis. Stakeholder interaction can also provide valuable information about sociocultural concerns such as historic, societal, environmental, geographic, conflicts, and cultural elements, and may guide the analyst to procure expert reports on key concerns such as environmental impact. Failing to identify and include stakeholders in the process can cause significant problems for the project.

Stakeholders may be individuals, groups, or entities (such as companies, organizations, and governments). A sample mapping of project stakeholders is shown below.

STAKEHOLDER ENGAGEMENT

Stakeholder engagement will typically occur at several milestones during the strategic project analysis process, especially during the early stages of the project such as objective definition and data collection. Interaction may take the form of interviews and meetings with key players, or group settings such as focus group discussions, workshops, community meetings, and surveys.

DOI: 10.4324/9781003014928-4

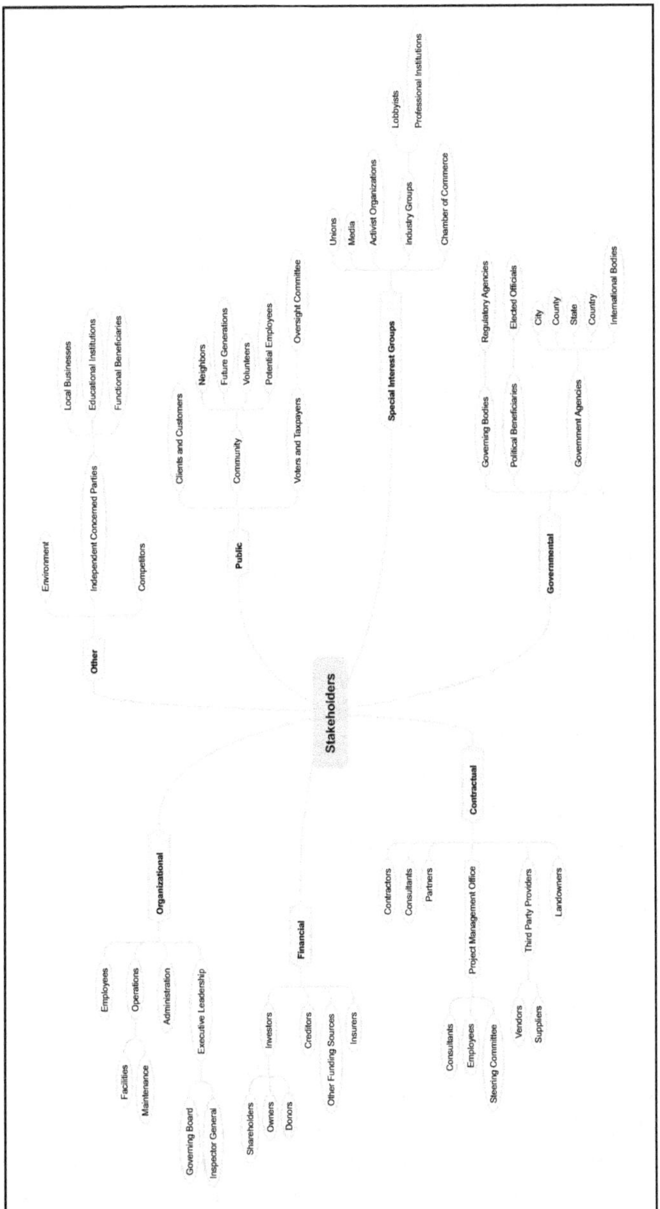

Figure 3.1 Stakeholder mind map

Source: Stakeholders – 2/25/16 – Mindjet

Once the analysis is completed, reporting to stakeholders is key to establishing and managing expectations. All stakeholder engagement activities should be well documented.

SUCCESS, FAILURE, AND VALUE

Once the project objective has been established, stakeholder input is crucial to the identification of performance requirements and potential outcomes, specifically benefits and disbenefits. This is because project stakeholders are those who define the very concepts of success, failure, and value.

As demonstrated in Figure 3.1, the list of project stakeholders is potentially broad and deep, and very diverse. Consequently, the definition of project success may vary for each stakeholder, leading to conflicting concepts of success; it is not unrealistic for a project to be both a success and a failure, from the stakeholder perspective. For this and other reasons, success is typically determined by those stakeholders who have standing.

STAKEHOLDER STANDING

Identifying and understanding stakeholders plays an even bigger role in strategic project analysis and evaluation practice when defining the scope of the analysis. The full population of internal and external entities that have a level of interest (stake) in or influence on a project can be quite large. Before engaging stakeholders in the analysis process and listing stakeholder-related costs and benefits, the analysis team needs to identify and understand who the project stakeholders are, and who has standing.

From a legal perspective, standing indicates a person's right to initiate a lawsuit, having been negatively impacted in some fashion. Similarly, in the context of strategic project analysis, stakeholder standing is achieved if benefits, disbenefits, or costs might accrue to the person. Standing indicates whose costs and benefits will be explicitly included in the analysis (and whose will be excluded). The identification of beneficiaries and negatively impacted populations is crucial to the analysis, requiring a description of all public and private entities likely to affect or be affected by the project.

As discussed in Chapter 2 of this book, the scope of strategic project analysis is typically limited to the impact area of (territory affected by) the proposed project and stakeholder beneficiaries within that area. Using geographic area to determine stakeholder standing is one way of maintaining objectivity, by avoiding bias associated with more granular identification and coding of populations within that boundary. However, if an understanding of potential distributional effects and equity is desired, a more detailed analysis of stakeholders is necessary which may include more granular population data such as: income, race, ethnicity, place of birth, age, religion, sex, gender, sexual orientation, political affiliation, veteran status, disability, family composition, occupation, and more. A distributional impact assessment can be conducted to identify how the scenario or intervention's positive and negative effects might vary (be distributed) across different categories of stakeholders.

Strategic project analysis may require consideration of stated or unstated obligations to these stakeholders, such as fiduciary duty, equity, cooperation, legitimization, and inclusion and diversity, especially when community values play an important role in decision-making and/or the project is expected to have long-term (generational) effects. The stakeholder identification process can be performed using relationship mapping, influence diagrams, logic models, and ranking.

There is always a risk of political involvement and influence in project planning, and critics of cost-benefit analysis believe it to be "an effective disguise for subjective advocacy"[1]. As such, it is crucial to identify power imbalances between stakeholders, and their level of involvement, degrees of interest and influence, urgency, political interests, and financial motivation.

ASSURANCE

Strategic project analysis, at its core, is intended to provide assurance (here defined[2] as reasonable confidence) that a project has been selected using rigorous, scientific methods that are accurate, complete, unbiased, verifiable, logical, and reproducible. Assurance is an organizational obligation to stakeholders that is closely related to accountability.

Assurance and accountability both assume cost-benefit analysis is unbiased and objective. Unfortunately, these conditions might not always be true, depending on the perspective and biases of the entity conducting the strategic project analysis. Optimism and cognitive delusion are common pitfalls in analysis, discussed further in Chapter 7 of this book.

REFLECTIONS AND EXERCISES

1. What methods might be used to identify stakeholders? Name at least five (5) and explain.
2. Identify fifteen (15) categories of stakeholders for a scenario in which a temporary field hospital is being established in another country.
3. What type of stakeholder obligations might be defined by a pre-existing contract? Name at least five (5) and explain.
4. What type of stakeholder obligations might result from societal norms? Name at least five (5) and explain.
5. What is the difference between assurance and accountability? Explain in your own words.
6. How can an organization explicitly provide assurance to stakeholders? Name at least five (5) and explain.

NOTES

1 Campen, J.T. (1986). *Benefit, Cost, and Beyond: The Political Economy of Benefit-Cost Analysis*, p. 52. Cambridge, MA: Ballinger.

2 Oxford English Dictionary Online. Retrieved on December 6, 2018 from https://en.oxforddictionaries.com/definition/assurance.

BIBLIOGRAPHY

Campen, J.T. (1986). *Benefit, Cost, and Beyond: The Political Economy of Benefit-Cost Analysis*. Cambridge, MA: Ballinger.

Green, S. and Sergeeva, N. (2019). Value Creation in Projects: Towards a Narrative Perspective. *International Journal of Project Management*, 37(5), 636–651.

Lock, D. (Ed.) (2021). *The Practitioner Handbook of Project Controls*. Abingdon: Routledge.

Nalewaik, A. and Mills, A. (2016). *Project Performance Review: Capturing the Value of Audit, Oversight, and Compliance for Project Success*. Abingdon: Routledge.

Oakes, G. (2008). *Project Reviews, Assurance, and Governance*. Aldershot: Gower Publishing.

Oxford English Dictionary Online. *Assurance*. Retrieved on December 6, 2018 from https://en.oxforddictionaries.com/definition/assurance

Sunstein, C. (2000). Cognition and Cost-Benefit Analysis. *The Journal of Legal Studies*, 29(S2): 1059–1103.

4

RISK

Risk identification and assessment can be used to evaluate a scenario's likelihood of achieving its stated objectives, by listing and then quantifying identified vulnerabilities, opportunities, and barriers to success. For the purposes of this book, risk is defined as a measurable likelihood of commercial or benefits loss associated with undertaking a scenario or maintaining the status quo. Although risk identification and treatment are not always included as part of cost-benefit analysis, they are elements of good governance and thus are discussed here.

Risk always exists and is always in flux, a consequence of action (and inaction). Risks may be interdependent or independent, objective or subjective, and they tend to multiply; risks that did not exist or were not known early in the project may appear or become known later in the project. For these reasons, risk management follows an iterative process of four steps: Identify, Quantify, Mitigate, and Monitor. This is a minor modification of the traditional Deming cycle (Plan, Do, Study, Act) for integrated learning and continuous improvement.

RISK IDENTIFICATION

The first phase of risk management is risk identification. A formal risk identification process may gather data from such sources as historic project information, lessons learned, expert opinion, stakeholder interviews, and a brainstorming workshop. SWOT (Strengths, Weaknesses, Opportunities, and Threats) analysis techniques may be used to identify positive and negative elements of the project, from which risks can be elicited.

DOI: 10.4324/9781003014928-5

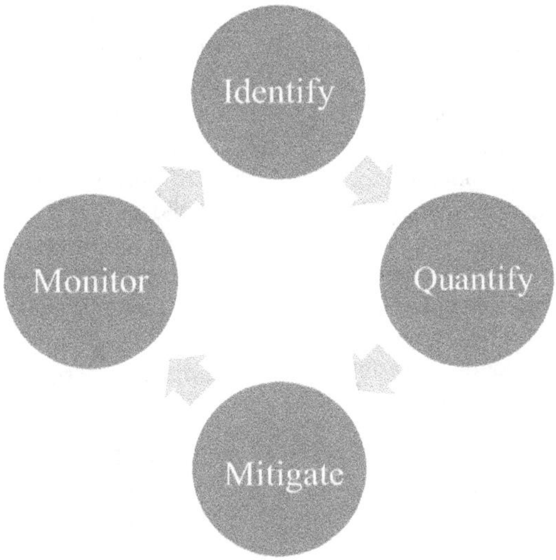

Figure 4.1 Modified Deming cycle

The output from the risk identification phase is a list of (unquantified) risks and disbenefits, in narrative format. The risk description may be stated in the form of a "risk bowtie" (Cause – Risk – Impact), which clarifies the root cause and potential impact of the risk.

Once identified, risks can be grouped into various categories. Some standard categories are shown below, with examples for each category.

Types of risk

Technical risks

- Proven/unproven technology
- New product development
- Implementation methodology
- Equipment and material performance
- Planning and design complexity
- Commissioning and testing
- Evolving requirements
- Tie-in to existing project or interface
- Scope change

- Engineering and design change
- Metric vs imperial measurement
- Differing standards
- Specialized equipment and materials
- Long-lead equipment
- Project in an operating facility
- Design conflict/interference
- Information systems
- Scalability
- Security vulnerabilities
- Technical complexity

Financial and economic risks

- Inflation
- Funding/financing
- Market forces
- Bidder perception of risk
- Labor and material costs and drivers
- Labor and material availability
- Interest rate
- Currency fluctuation
- Bankruptcy
- Alternative approaches to insurance

Statutory and political risks

- Local law or government policy
- Government influence on disputes
- Environmental regulations
- Property acquisition
- Permitting
- External stakeholder influence
- Testing and certification
- Official and unofficial holidays
- Religious observance
- Customs (import/export)
- Visas (immigration)

Organizational risks

- Project team capability
- Contractor failure
- Contractor/vendor/consultant failure or default
- Mergers and acquisitions
- Staff turnover
- Stakeholder turnover
- Degree of unfamiliarity
- Schedule acceleration
- Gaps in responsibility or scope
- Communication
- Executive support of project
- Business processes
- Delegated authority
- Organizational culture
- Reputation

Contractual risks

- Contractual liability
- Warranties
- Liquidated/consequential/punitive damages
- Construction defect
- Risk transfer
- Conflicting contract language

- Inadequate contract protections
- Intellectual property
- New contract/delivery method

Other risks

- Climate
- Safety
- Unknown conditions
- Archaeological findings
- Contamination
- Local customs
- Infrastructure
- Theft
- Translation error
- Productivity
- Competition

The number of risks per category will depend on the type of project that is being analyzed, the location, financing type, contract and project delivery type, and organizational structure. For example, manufacturing, construction, innovation, scientific, and high tech projects may have a high number of technical risks. International projects may have economic, cultural, and political risks.

RISK ANALYSIS

The "Quantify" phase of risk management is the risk analysis itself. During this step, the risks are analyzed and assigned values for probability (stated as a percentage), cost impact (typically stated in dollars), and schedule impact (typically stated in months). This type of analysis relies on professional judgment, in which objectivity and independence are implicit characteristics; a discussion of these concepts can be found in Chapter 7 of this book.

Once risks have been quantified, they can be ranked in severity from high to low, representing the degree of consequences to project and corporate objectives and, thus, the amount of management attention the risks will attract.

RISK MITIGATION

The "Mitigate" phase of risk management refers to risk treatment. During this effort, a risk owner is assigned to each risk, and specific action items are identified to mitigate (reduce) the risk. Deadlines may be established for each action item.

There are four categories of risk treatment: transfer, avoidance, reduction, and acceptance. Risk transfer to another party is most often accomplished through a contractual arrangement or insurance. Avoidance means undertaking mitigation actions to reduce the probability to zero, such that the risk does not occur. Reduction is accomplished by reducing the potential impacts and probability of the risk, but not to zero. Risk acceptance is managed by adding contingency funds to the budget, without undertaking mitigation actions.

Mitigation activities are expected to help reduce or even eliminate (avoid) the probability of a risk occurring and its impact should it occur. It is possible to have an initial risk treatment plan of reduction, then shift to risk acceptance once the risk has been reduced to an acceptable level.

RISK MANAGEMENT

The fourth phase of risk management focuses on monitoring. Project risks are dynamic and constantly changing as the project progresses, so their probability and impact fluctuate. Periodic risk review is necessary and may be scheduled for specific time intervals, stage gates, or project milestones.

The dynamic nature of risk also means that old risks may be closed, and new risks identified. Thus, the risk cycle returns to its starting point, the identification of new risks. Next, both the new and old risks are analyzed. Risks that have been mitigated can be closed. The new risks are quantified, and the quantification of old risks is reviewed and modified as needed. The new risks are assigned a risk owner and action items, and the action items for old risks are reviewed and updated or closed as required. New action items may be added. Next, it's back to the start of the risk cycle. Lather, rinse, repeat.

OPPORTUNITY

Where there are risks, there are also elements that are the opposite of risk (also considered positive risks). Opportunity can be defined as a measurable likelihood of commercial or benefits gain associated with undertaking a scenario or maintaining the status quo.

As with risk, there are four categories of opportunity treatment, which are themselves opposites of the four categories of risk treatment: share, exploitation, enhancement, and acceptance. Opportunities may be shared within an organization or with external parties. Exploiting an opportunity means undertaking actions to increase its probability to 100 per cent to make it occur. Enhancing an opportunity means increasing its potential impact and probability, in an attempt to maximize its effect. Opportunity acceptance is achieved by allowing the opportunity to occur, without undertaking mitigation actions.

RISK IN ECONOMIC ANALYSIS

All decision-making is conducted under a certain degree of uncertainty. Risk represents activity that might or might not occur within the scenario whereas a base scenario is limited to costs and benefits that are fully expected to occur. Because the best-case (most profitable) scenario is typically modeled in traditional economic analysis, formal risk identification and analysis are often excluded during the early phases of an iterative financial cost-benefit analysis process.

Risk identification or analysis may be provided as an appendix to the analysis instead of being treated as an integral part of the cost-benefit calculations, with the understanding that the risk list may be treated as a separate component during the decision-making process. The risk list will also be useful during project execution, and any statistical risk models can be used later to measure the confidence level in the project and help establish cost contingency and schedule float. If risks are excluded from the analysis, that omission should be noted in the analysis documentation.

Ex-post strategic project analysis, in capturing actual realized costs and benefits, will necessarily also include any risks and/or opportunities that have occurred.

RISK IN SOCIETAL VALUE ANALYSIS

However, the core of program evaluation, as applied in cost-effectiveness analysis, impact evaluation, benefit-cost analysis, objectives-based evaluation, and other approaches, is predicated on strategic risk concepts. In these analyses, risks are defined in the context of societal benefits or disbenefits such as loss of life, health effects, environmental impact, and more. Projects are conceptualized, and objectives established, specifically to combat or prevent such current or future risks. These outcomes are typically quantified using a monetary proxy, well-being units, or an ordinal scale as discussed in Chapter 2 of this book, and may be based on average numbers and statistical probabilities. Such projects typically have long time horizons, requiring ongoing risk management over a time frame of years, decades, or more.

It is important to make a distinction between current or future risks in the context of society, sustainability, and resilience, for which such projects are undertaken, and project-specific risks that represent a threat to the completion of the project. For this type of project, project-specific risk impacts may be quantified and compared against the quantified expected benefits.

$$Benefit - Risk\,Ratio = \frac{Total\ Benefits}{Total\ Risk\ Impact}$$

Equation 4.1 Benefit-risk ratio

The benefit-risk ratio should be greater than one for an acceptable undertaking, whether that be a project or merely an action. Some organizations may calculate the risk-benefit ratio, which is the inverse of Equation 4.1; for that calculation, the ideal ratio should be less than one. Benefits and risks should be stated as present value.

REFLECTIONS AND EXERCISES

1 Name five (5) types of risk (not already named) that might be quantified using welfare economics methods. Explain why and how they might be quantified.
2 Find three (3) examples of monetary proxy for societal benefits or disbenefits. Cite your sources.
3 Identify twenty (20) types of risk for a scenario in which a new manufacturing plant is being constructed in Puerto Rico.

4 Using your own words, explain why sensitivity testing is a type of risk analysis.
5 When you make decisions, how sensitive are you to risk? Explain and provide two (2) examples.

BIBLIOGRAPHY

Dudley, S., Pérez, D., Mannix, B., and Carrigan, C. (2019). Dynamic Benefit-Cost Analysis for Uncertain Futures. *Journal of Benefit Cost Analysis*, 10(2): 206–225.

Hollmann, J. (2019). *Project Risk Quantification: A Practitioner's Guide to Realistic Cost and Schedule Risk Management*. Houston, TX: Probabilistic Publishing.

Lock, D. (Ed.) (2021). *The Practitioner Handbook of Project Controls*. Abingdon: Routledge.

Morgan, M.G. Morgan and Henrion, M. (1990). *Uncertainty: A Guide to Dealing with Uncertainty in Quantitative Risk and Policy Analysis*. Cambridge: Cambridge University Press.

Nalewaik, A. and Mills, A. (2016). *Project Performance Review: Capturing the Value of Audit, Oversight, and Compliance for Project Success*. Abingdon: Routledge.

Sunstein, C., (2000). Cognition and Cost-Benefit Analysis. *The Journal of Legal Studies*, 29(S2): 1059–1103.

The W. Edwards Deming Institute. *The PDSA Cycle*. Retrieved on March 23, 2024 from https://deming.org/explore/pdsa.

5

QUANTITATIVE CONCEPTS

Tangible costs and benefits can be counted, and thus valued. The most common method of strategic project analysis is cost-benefit analysis, in which costs and benefits are valued in monetary terms. Quantitative methods are used when an economic justification for scenario selection is preferred or required. Many of the concepts discussed here are used to measure economic attractiveness.

Several data points are key to economic analysis and necessary to the quantitative process. These are:

- The timeline (schedule) for the proposed scenario, measured as the total number of interest periods (n), usually stated in years
- The expected timing of expenditures and receivable line items (cash flow)
- The assumed interest rate or discount rate percentage (i), a percentage usually stated as annual interest; in mathematical calculations, the value of x% is entered as x/100
- Estimated values for itemized costs and benefits, as discussed in Chapter 2 of this book

An observation about quantitative concepts: there are a certain number of variables in strategic project analysis. Typically, those are: investment costs, future benefits, future costs, future disbenefits, and future revenue. It is safe to say that, as project analysis practices have evolved over time, a "Wild West" mentality has emerged in which different disciplines have managed to regard, disregard, and combine those variables in many similar but slightly different and not quite infinite ways. Financial/economic analysis still tends to focus

DOI: 10.4324/9781003014928-6

exclusively on costs and revenue, whereas evaluation/social value practice still tends to focus near-exclusively on benefits and disbenefits. As mentioned in Chapter 2 of this book, evaluation methods may choose to omit the time value of money, and may use total benefits in calculations instead of net benefits. Slight variations in equations can yield different results and thus can influence the selection of scenarios; as such, the selection and use of equations may surface bias and ethical issues. Emphasizing what was said earlier: If simplification of equations is preferred, the analyst should perform both the original and simplified calculations, and then compare them as part of the sensitivity testing exercise.

The terminology used in analysis is often conflicting. The author has even seen "inputs" used to mean either money and resources put into the project or revenue and benefits received from the project, and "outputs" to mean either money and resources spent on the project or benefits and revenue received from the project. For that very reason, such terms have been avoided in this book, and clarifications have been added to note where conflicting terminology or variations on equations might occur.

When applying any equations, first make sure the methodology shown and terminology used is appropriate for your purpose and discipline. Reiterating Chapter 2 of this book, all equations, acronyms, and terminology used in strategic project analysis should be described in detail as part of analysis documentation, and any omissions from (or additions to) those equations noted.

Cost is frequently not considered in social project evaluations, or may be mentioned but not analyzed. Whether this is due to a lack of available funding for a comprehensive analysis, the evaluator's discomfort with maths, lack of training, distaste for the politics of funding, or a lack of accessible quantitative methods is difficult to determine. In evaluation practice, "the number of effectiveness or outcomes studies still far outweighs the number of cost-inclusive evaluations."[1] Indeed, in an examination of 117 evaluation studies, only six studies (5 percent) were found to mention cost[2]. Even when cost was considered, other research concluded that (when the program evaluated exceeded a duration of one year) some fifty percent (50 percent) of evaluation studies did not apply time value of money calculations during quantification[3]. This is an unfortunate defect in the practice and profession of evaluation.

This book advocates for including cost in project analysis because available funding is never infinite; analysis from a business and cost feasibility perspective is necessary. Whether explicitly stated or not, the cost and continuation of any undertaking are always factors in decision-making. Every resource invested in an endeavor has a cost, including time and "free" components such as donated supplies, services, and equipment, volunteers, and interns. This book also advocates for including the time value of money in calculations, except for very long-term and generational benefits.

CASH FLOW

Cash flow is used not just in strategic project analysis but also in capital budgeting. Cash flow may be represented as a table, as shown in the example below.

Cash flow may also be represented as a diagram, as shown in the example below.

In the cash flow diagram shown above in Figure 5.1, the initial equipment and annual repair costs from Table 5.1 are added together as expenses, and the annual revenue and end-of-life salvage values from Table 5.1 are added together as income.

PRESENT VALUE

In a traditional economic analysis, the sum total of costs and benefits are usually stated in "present value" (P) amounts. Not only is this simplest from an estimating perspective because supporting

Table 5.1 Cash flow table

Time (Years)	*Equipment Cost ($K)*	*Repair Cost ($K)*	*Revenue ($K)*	*Salvage Value ($K)*
0 (Today)	10,000			
1		1,000	3,000	
2		1,000	3,000	
3		1,000	3,000	
4		1,000	3,000	
5		1,000	3,000	3,000

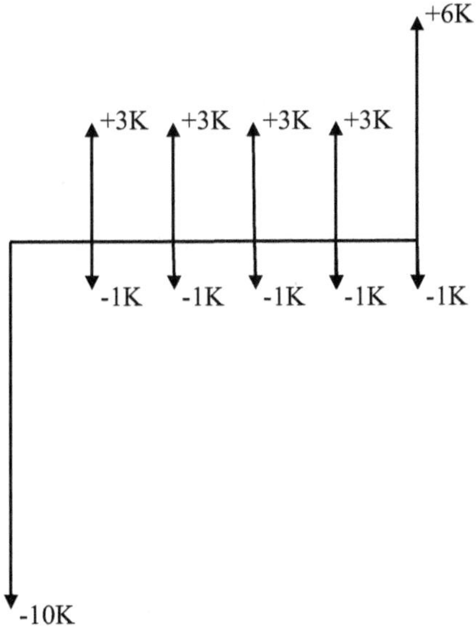

Figure 5.1 Cash flow diagram

documentation likely relies on currently published pricing or quotes, but it is also most easily comprehended by the audience. People think in contemporary terms, so costs stated in present-day terms are relatable and relative, and they can readily be compared to the actual or perceived cost of other tangible items or activities. Further, stating all costs and benefits in present-day terms is one way of enabling comparison between costs, benefits, and entire scenarios that have different durations, using a common denominator.

Symbols and mathematical notation

The symbols and mathematical notations used in quantitative analysis are not universal and tend to vary by profession or sector (such as finance, economics, health, evaluation, and engineering). P may be described as PV, F as FV, i as r (especially when using both consumption and investment rates in the analysis, or a weighted average w), A as R, n as t, etc. The equations, however, always maintain the same format and structure.

Equation format

There are differences in format and mathematical notation that may make the equations look different, even though they are technically the same in structure. For example, a simple way of writing the Present Value equation (discussed in more detail soon) is this:

$$P = F/(1+i)^n$$

Equation 5.1 Present value (simple notation)

A mathematician might write the same thing this way, instead:

$$P = \frac{F}{(1+i)^n}$$

Equation 5.2 Present value (mathematical notation)

And, if you are typing the present value calculation into a spreadsheet using a mathematical formula, you would write it this way:

$$P = F/(1+i)^\wedge n$$

Equation 5.3 Present value (spreadsheet notation)

In the spreadsheet formula, F is the address (known as a cell name) of the cell (such as B5, or A1) where Future Value is entered, i is the cell name where the interest rate per period is entered, and n is the cell name where the number of periods in an annuity is entered.

But if you are using the Present Value function in Microsoft Excel, you would write it this way:

$$P = \text{PV}(\text{rate, nper, pmt, [fv], [type]})$$

Equation 5.4 Present value (Microsoft Excel notation)

Microsoft Excel Help includes very descriptive notes for automated formulas, which define each element of the function, with additional remarks and guidance. The Help functionality makes it easy to write the formula in a step-by-step fashion.

Each of these four approaches are different ways of writing the same equation, and will generate the same answer. It doesn't matter which style of notation makes most sense to you. Mathematical notation is used in this book.

There is no shortage of books available on the topic of quantitative concepts in economic analysis, most of which are tailored to a specific discipline or field of practice. There is no one "best" book or symbol or notation, and no single entity or organization "owns" the core quantitative methods and equations. The equations in this book are meant to be a simplified introduction to the mathematical concepts of strategic project analysis, from which the reader can graduate to more in-depth and industry-specific exploration of the topic.

INTEREST RATE AND DISCOUNT RATE

Time and money are interrelated. The value of money changes with time ("time value") owing to its earning potential; money invested (known as capital) can generate (or lose) revenue. However, that earning potential may also be offset by the cost of interest for monies borrowed and changes in purchasing power owing to inflation, which can be unpredictable. For analysis purposes, it is usually assumed adequate funds will be available, and money invested will always gain value. Any uncertainty surrounding funding and money invested is addressed as part of the risk analysis process.

An interest rate is used in financial time value of money calculations, using rate information from financial markets to represent the expected return on investments (ROI). The investment rate of interest used for private sector investment may include taxes to be paid on the interest earned, and thus may be higher than the market interest rate.

In an analysis that considers societal benefits, a discount rate is used in the time value of money calculations that reflects the value of today's benefits compared to the value of future benefits. Discounting is the reverse of compounding interest. Discount rates are typically higher than interest rates, owing to their composition, but are applied in the same way using the same equations; i is used for both interest and discount rates. The selection of discount rate is critical and can make or break the analysis, with the potential to significantly influence one scenario over another. When the scenarios have long durations, future and generational benefits become discounted to far below current benefits. This is a known ethical problem with discounting. There is a school of thought that advocates for the use of a declining discount rate or a discount rate of zero for environmental projects to preserve the value of far-future (100-year) benefits, reduce bias toward the present, and collectively mitigate existential threats.

Selecting an appropriate rate for the purposes of analysis is complicated owing to ever-fluctuating market-driven rates and inflation, and the rate naturally becomes less accurate each year owing to the challenge of forecasting market impacts, making it particularly problematic for long-term analyses. The rate is, ultimately, conceptual and will vary between public (societal) and private (corporate) projects, reflecting differences in opportunity costs. Governmental guidance for the selection of discount rate changes over time, reflecting constantly changing philosophies. Two different rates could be used, which requires separating consumption and investment for calculation (with a predictably significant impact on the analysis results). The most recent US Government recommendation is for the use of a single social discount rate, reversing previous guidance[4].

Options and proxies include: prevailing investment interest rates (SOC, or social opportunity cost of capital), market interest rates that consider the shadow price of capital, social rate of time preference (SRTP) which reflects equity issues and sustainability, discount rates that include risks and uncertainty, declining discount rate (hyperbolic discounting), weighted average cost of capital (WACC) that reflects corporate investors' desired rate of return, and many more. The selection of rate may be controversial. Of these approaches, SOC and SRTP are the most common.

As part of strategic project analysis documentation, the choice of rate should be thoroughly documented and well justified, made as transparent as possible for the report audience. Sensitivity analysis should be conducted several times, using different rates and a rate of zero to test scenario reactivity to changes in rate.

FUTURE VALUE

The future value (F or FV) of an investment is described by the following equation:

$$F = P(1+i)^n$$

Equation 5.5 Future value

In the equation above, F is the future value, P is the present value, i is the interest rate, and n is the number of periods. For hard-keyed calculation in a spreadsheet, the formula would be written as = P*(1+i)^n, each variable referencing the cell addresses by column and row (such as B5, or A1) containing the variables P, i, and n. However, there is a simpler method. Microsoft Excel users can apply pre-programmed financial functions for this and all other cost-benefit analysis calculations. The future value function syntax in Microsoft Excel is FV(rate,nper,pmt,PV,type), where rate is the interest (i), nper is the number of payment periods (n), pmt is a recurring payment per period (R or A) discussed next, PV is the present value P, and "type" indicates whether payments are due at the end of the period (0) or at the beginning of the period (1). These variables and terminology are typical for all Microsoft Excel financial functions.

At the very beginning of the time series, when the investment P has just been made, n=0 and P=F, expressed as $P(1+i)^0$. The equation $(1+i)^0$ equals 1, no matter what interest rate (i) is used, because the exponent is zero (0). At the end of the first period, when interest has been earned for the first time, future value is calculated as the present value plus the interest earned, which is written as F = P + iP. This equation can be simplified to P(1+i), also written as $P(1+i)^1$. At the end of the second period, when interest has again been earned, its value becomes P(1+i)(1+i), which is also written as $P(1+i)^2$, and so forth.

In the equation above, the interest rate and periods are stated in years, with interest compounding annually. Should interest be compounded quarterly (four times per year), monthly (12 times per year), or daily (365 times per year), the variables will need to be adjusted accordingly, dividing i by the number of compounding periods per year (lower case p) and multiplying n by the number of compounding periods per year (p), as shown below. This is typical for all financial formulas in this book chapter.

$$F = P(1+\tfrac{i}{p})^{np}$$

Equation 5.6 Future value (compounded interest version)

The formula for future value using a simple interest rate (in which interest on a loan is calculated once annually on the original amount P, instead of calculating interest periodically on both the original amount P + any interest that has already accumulated) is F = P(1+in). Personal loans and coupon-paying bonds often utilize simple interest, as do calculations where the period is less than one year. Most economic analyses, lines of credit, bank accounts, and business investments use the compound interest formula, not simple interest.

For the purposes of calculating present value, determining interest rate, or seeking the number of periods for which the mathematical statement is true, the above equation can be manipulated to perform those computations. In fact, almost every economic analysis formula can be said to be derived from Equation 5.1. By adjusting the formula to move P to the left side of the equation, the present value can be described by:

$$P = \frac{F}{(1+i)^n}$$

Equation 5.7 Present value

The present value function syntax in Microsoft Excel is PV(rate, nper, pmt, FV, type).

The total interest earned (I) is stated as I = F–P.

BENEFIT–COST RATIO

In evaluation practice, the benefit–cost ratio (BCR) is calculated to gauge the attractiveness of an investment, with the goal of creating benefits that exceed the investment costs. It is very similar to the calculation for ROI, except it includes quantified nonfinancial benefits and disbenefits. This is one of the two most common calculations in public project analysis and evaluation, the other being cost-effectiveness analysis, discussed in Chapter 6 of this book.

$$BCR = \frac{Benefits - Disbenefits}{Cost}$$

Equation 5.8 Benefit-cost ratio

For a feasible project, the ratio should be greater than one (B/C > 1) because the sum of expected benefits should exceed the sum of planned costs. For societal projects, the ratio represents the project's contribution to government or organizational policy objectives.

Note that approaches to this calculation sometimes vary in practice, and it has been well abused. The costs shown in the denominator might be only the initial investment cost, instead of total costs. An incremental BCR might also be calculated. As with ROI (discussed in Chapter 2 of this book), the computation may be performed without first stating all variables as present values, but the results using this approach will be very approximate and, thus, less accurate.

ANNUITY PAYMENT

Not all costs and benefits occur at one single fixed point in time. An annuity payment is a uniform (constant) recurring payment that is made at the end of each time period, for a certain number of time periods. Its relationship to present value is described mathematically as:

$$P = A\frac{(1+i)^n - 1}{i(1+i)^n}$$

Equation 5.9 Present value (annuity payment version)

The annuity payment is shown in the above formula as A. Using the formula above, recurring costs and benefits can be stated in "present value" terms and included in the cost-benefit analysis.

Stating all costs and benefits as an equivalent annual amount is another way to compare equipment lives and entire scenarios that have different durations. The formula is written as:

$$A = P\frac{i(1+i)^n}{(1+i)^n - 1}$$

Equation 5.10 Future value (annuity payment version)

The annuity payment (also known as annual worth) function is a shortcut to discounting each year's cost and benefits separately and then adding them together. The syntax for the annuity payment function in Microsoft Excel is PMT(rate, nper, PV, FV, type).

NET PRESENT VALUE

Net present value is one of the two most common calculations in financial analysis, the other being ROI, discussed in Chapter 2 of this book. Net present value (NPV) is the algebraic difference between discounted benefits and discounted costs, if they were to happen today. Stated another way, NPV is the difference between the present value of all quantified outcomes, and the present value of all costs (including investment costs). It omits nonquantifiable outcomes. Each item added or subtracted must be stated in present value.

$$NPV = Benefits - Disbenefits - Costs$$

Equation 5.11 Net present value

A positive NPV or an NPV of zero means the scenario is financially viable. The net present value calculation is identical to the B-C calculation described in Chapter 2 of this book, stated in present value amounts. NPV is often used to compare mutually exclusive projects. NPV is also used in conjunction with other quantitative approaches to determine scenario viability, and is a test used to accept or reject a scenario before continuing with analysis.

PROFITABILITY INDEX

The profitability index (PI), also known as the Present Worth Index, Profit Investment Ratio, or Present Value Index, uses present values to calculate the value per dollar (resource unit) invested. This is a purely financial calculation that does not consider benefits and disbenefits. It is similar to the computation for ROI.

There are two possible approaches to the PI calculation. One excludes the initial investment cost in the calculation of NPV, considering only future cash flows. The other approach includes the initial investment cost in the calculation of NPV but then adds it back in:

$$PI = \frac{Net\ Present\ Value\ of\ Future\ Cash\ Flows}{Initial\ Investment\ Cost}$$

Equation 5.12 Profitability Index

$$PI = \frac{Net\ present\ Value + Initial\ Investment\ Cost}{Initial\ Investment\ Cost}$$

Equation 5.13 Profitability Index

The results will be identical for both calculations because the NPV calculation deducts the present value of the initial investment; adding that amount back into the calculation brings the initial investment cost influence on the calculation to zero, which is the same as excluding the initial investment cost and focusing only on future cash flows.

In practice, PI might also be (erroneously) referred to as internal rate of return (discussed next) or the discounted cash flow rate of return. For a feasible project, the ratio will be greater than one (PI > 1), as will NPV (NPV > 1), because the two calculations are closely related.

INTERNAL RATE OF RETURN

The internal rate of return (IRR) is a calculation of how much a project earns per time period, stated as a percentage per year. It should be greater than the minimum acceptable rate of return (which may be the interest charged on borrowed money, known as the cost of capital, and/or the inflation rate) in order for a scenario to be viable. IRR is the interest rate, also known as the discount rate, at which NPV equals zero. IRR states growth as an annual rate of return, whereas ROI calculates total return; despite this, IRR may sometimes be referred to as ROI. The internal rate of return is a measure of the attractiveness of a scenario; private projects may be measured against a specific IRR benchmark (such as the WACC), required rate of return, or minimum acceptable rate of return (also designated as i*). The internal rate of return is most often used for investment and financial decision-making.

IRR can be calculated using the present value equation to solve for the discount rate, or the IRR formula in Microsoft Excel, but is most easily determined by graphing present value (P) against interest rate (*i*), and finding the intersection where P = 0. It cannot be used if multiple discount rates are applied to the scenario, or if the scenario's cash flow is variable and complicated. IRR is used in conjunction with other quantitative approaches to determine scenario viability, and is a test used to accept or reject a scenario before continuing with analysis. The IRR can be found by graphing the data shown in Table 5.2 above, with an approximate result of 6.9 percent.

Table 5.2 Example 1

FV ($K)	*Time (Years)*	*3.00%*	*5.00%*	*7.00%*	*9.00%*	*6.90%*
-10,000.00		-10,000.00	-10,000.00	-10,000.00	-10,000.00	-10,000.00
1,000.00	1.00	970.87	952.38	934.58	917.43	935.44
1,000.00	2.00	942.60	907.03	873.44	841.68	875.04
1,000.00	3.00	915.14	863.84	816.30	772.18	818.54
1,000.00	4.00	888.49	822.70	762.90	708.43	765.70
1,000.00	5.00	862.61	783.53	712.99	649.93	716.26
2,000.00	6.00	1,674.97	1,492.43	1,332.68	1,192.53	1,340.03
2,000.00	7.00	1,626.18	1,421.36	1,245.50	1,094.07	1,253.51
2,000.00	8.00	1,578.82	1,353.68	1,164.02	1,003.73	1,172.58
2,000.00	9.00	1,532.83	1,289.22	1,087.87	920.86	1,096.88
2,000.00	10.00	1,488.19	1,227.83	1,016.70	844.82	1,026.06
	NPV	**$2,480.70**	**$1,113.99**	**($53.03)**	**($1,054.34)**	**$0.04**
	IRR	**3%**	**5%**	**7%**	**9%**	6.90%

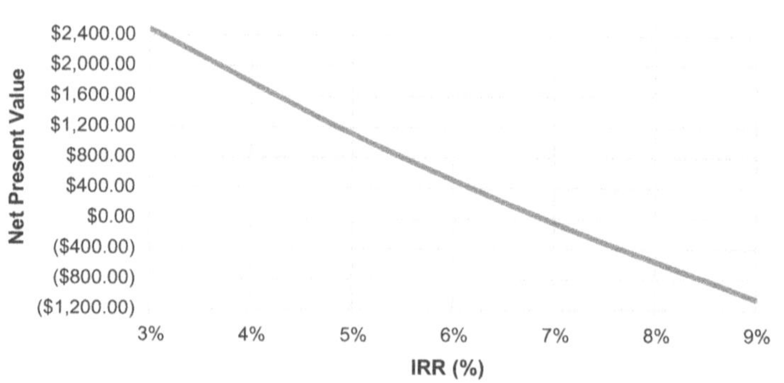

Figure 5.2 IRR graph

BREAK-EVEN POINT

Break-even analysis identifies the financial point at which a scenario has recovered its initial investment, where total cost equals total revenue (benefits). Like IRR, this payback period can be determined both through calculation and graphing, yielding a breakeven volume answer in sales, production, or service units. When combined with cash flow planning, break-even analysis can be used to determine the point in time (payback period) after which the scenario begins making a profit. A common goal for corporate break-even timing is six to eighteen months, but may be still be acceptable even as long as five years.

The data shown in Table 5.2, with i = 8%, can also be shown as a graph (see Figure 5.3, below), with the break-even point at approximately three-and-a-half years.

Information required for the break-even point (Q, in units) calculation includes fixed costs (F_c), variable costs per unit (V_c), and unit price (sales price per unit, U_p):

$$Q = F_c / \left(U_p - V_c\right)$$

Equation 5.14 Break-even point (units)

When the above equation uses present values, the result is called the Discounted Payback Period.

Fixed costs are overhead costs that are constant, such as building rent, basic utility services, corporate advertising, insurance, and corporate salaries. Variable costs per unit are the specific costs related to producing the unit, which vary proportionately with the volume of units produced, such as direct materials and labor, utilities and advertising related to goods produced, packing supplies and shipping, and manufacturing salaries.

Unlike IRR, break-even analysis does not consider the time value of money and cannot be used to analyze long-term profitability because it does not consider costs and benefits that occur beyond the payback period. It is most often used in corporate scenarios, to determine the number of units (or services) that need to be produced or sold to recoup associated costs and make a profit. Break-even analysis is used in conjunction with other quantitative approaches to determine scenario viability and is a test used to accept or reject a scenario before continuing with analysis. If a scenario has

Table 5.3 Example 2

Time (Years)	*Equipment Cost ($K)*	*Repair Cost ($K)*	*Revenue ($K)*	*Salvage Value ($K)*	*Sum*	*P*	*Time (Years)*	*Running total*
0 (Today)	15,000				-15,000.00	-15,000.00		-15,000.00
1		1,000	6,000		5,000.00	4,629.63	1.00	-10,370.37
2		1,000	6,000		5,000.00	4,286.69	2.00	-6,083.68
3		1,000	6,000		5,000.00	3,969.16	3.00	-2,114.52
4		1,000	6,000		5,000.00	3,675.15	4.00	1,560.63
5		1,000	6,000	5,000	10,000.00	6,805.83	5.00	8,366.47

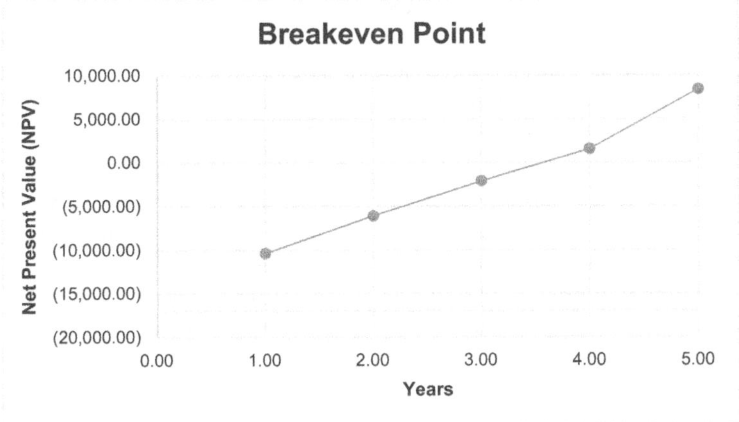

Figure 5.3 Break-even point graph

no break-even point, it might not be automatically rejected if additional justification can prove the planned outcomes are worth the investment. For government services scenarios, break-even analysis may be used to determine when surplus funds will become available for other uses, or tailor unit pricing (such as sliding-scale fees) to minimize surplus funds.

LIFE-CYCLE COST

Lifecycle cost analysis (LCCA) is a specialized type of CBA often used for manufacturing and infrastructure construction scenarios that considers all the costs incurred owing to ownership of an asset. It is also known as a total cost of ownership analysis. The whole lifecycle cost of a scenario offers a more comprehensive understanding of the scenario than a typical scope-limited cost-benefit analysis. Comparing the lifecycle costs of different scenarios provides valuable insight into tradeoffs between initial investment cost and the cost of ongoing operations, and may thus yield a different result than a traditional CBA.

The lifecycle cost calculation includes all costs related to the acquisition or design & construction of the project, operations and optimized maintenance costs over the asset's useful life, and any decommissioning or disposal costs or salvage benefits. Useful life is usually assigned as the MACRS[5] depreciation definition for various kinds of assets, ranging from 3 to 39 years. However, public works projects, which in practice have a near-infinite life, may be analyzed over a maximum of 50 years.

Lifecycle cost-benefit analysis (LCCBA) is a related type of analysis that uses a circular economy and cradle-to-cradle approach to the analysis scope. Essentially, an LCCBA is an LCCA that includes (utilizing shadow pricing) user costs and, increasingly, environmental and societal costs and benefits.

It is worth noting that errors in quantification and forecasting are amplified by long timeframes for analysis owing to lack of data and uncertainties related to inflation and other variables.

REAL OPTIONS

A real options approach to strategic project analysis (real options analysis) considers a scenario in which an initial investment is made in order to create an opportunity for an even more profitable future investment, without committing the organization to that future investment at the present time. This permits some flexibility in future decision-making. The future investment(s) may be a new project, an expansion of a pilot project or small-scale project to full scale, or the next stage of a stage-gate funded project. Other real options include temporarily stopping, postponing (deferring), or permanently abandoning a project, scaling down a project, and changing the project to yield different expected benefits or outcomes (such as societal value or manufactured product).

The real option may be one of several scenarios considered for analysis, compared to other scenarios such as the cost of proceeding immediately with a full-scale project.

PROBLEMS, REFLECTIONS, AND EXERCISES

1. If you invest $1,000 today at an interest rate of 8 percent per year, how much will the investment be worth in five years? Perform the calculation twice, once using the equation and once using Microsoft Excel.
2. Calculate the net present value for the scenario shown in Table 5.1 and Figure 5.1, at an interest rate of 5 percent per year.
3. Draw a cash flow diagram for the following scenario:

Time (Years)	*Project Management ($K)*	*Warehouse Cost ($K)*	*Construction ($K)*	*Engineering ($K)*	*Equipment ($K)*	*Revenue ($K)*	*Out*	*In*
0 (Today)	960	20	0	2,600	0	0	3,580	
1	960	5	1,000	930	16,000	0	18,895	
2	960	5	4,000	1,300	14,400	0	20,665	
3	960	5	780	1,500	13,500	0	16,745	
4	960	5	300	1,300	20,900	0	23,465	
5						20,000		20000
6						20,000		20000
7						25,000		25000
8						25,000		25000
9						25,000		25000
10						25,000		25000

4. Find three (3) examples of different discount rates used in cost-benefit analyses. Cite your sources.
5. How might the future value equation be useful to you in real life? Provide two (2) examples.
6. How might the annuity payment equation be useful to you in real life? Provide two (2) examples.

NOTES

1 Herman, P.M., Avery, D.J., Schemp, C.S., and Walsh, M.E. (2009). Are Cost-Inclusive Evaluations Worth the Effort? *Evaluation and Program Planning*, 32: 55–61.
2 Christie, C.A. and Fleischer, D.N. (2010). Insight Into Evaluation Practice: A Content Analysis of Designs and Methods Used in Evaluation Studies Published in North American Evaluation-Focused Journals. *American Journal of Evaluation*, 31(3): 326–346.
3 Madsen, L.B., Eddleston, M. Hansen, K.S., & Konradsen, F. (2017). Quality Assessment of Economic Evaluations of Suicide and Self-Harm Interventions: A Systematic Review. *Crisis*, 1–14.
4 See U.S. EPA and U.S. OMB guidance.
5 Department of the Treasury (2022). *Publication 946 (Cat. No. 13081F): How to Depreciate Property*. Washington, DC: Internal Revenue Service

BIBLIOGRAPHY

Campen, J.T. (1986). *Benefit, Cost, and Beyond: The Political Economy of Benefit Cost Analysis*. Cambridge, MA: Ballinger.

Christie, C.A. and Fleischer, D.N. (2010). Insight Into Evaluation Practice: A Content Analysis of Designs and Methods Used in Evaluation Studies Published in North American Evaluation-Focused Journals. *American Journal of Evaluation*, 31(3): 326–346.

Department of the Treasury (2022). *How to Depreciate Property.* Publication 946, Cat. No. 13081F. Washington, DC: Internal Revenue Service.

Government Accountability Office (2018). *Assessment Methodology for Economic Analysis.* GAO-18–151SP. Washington, DC: United States Government Accountability Office.

Green, S. and Sergeeva, N. (2019). Value Creation in Projects: Towards a Narrative Perspective. *International Journal of Project Management*, 37(5): 636–651.

Herman, P.M., Avery, D.J., Schemp, C.S., and Walsh, M.E. (2009). Are Cost-Inclusive Evaluations Worth the Effort? *Evaluation and Program Planning*, 32: 55–61.

IEEE (2023). *IEEE Technology and Engineering Management Society Body of Knowledge (TEMSBOK)*. Hoboken, NJ: Wiley-IEEE Press.

Lock, D. (Ed.) (2021). *The Practitioner Handbook of Project Controls*. Abingdon: Routledge.

Madsen, L.B., Eddleston, M. Hansen, K.S. & Konradsen, F. (2017). Quality Assessment of Economic Evaluations of Suicide and Self-Harm Interventions: A Systematic Review. *Crisis,* 39(2): 82–95.

Office of Management and Budget (November 9, 2023). *Circular No. A-4, Regulatory Analysis*. Washington, DC: Executive Office of the President.

Office of Management and Budget (November 9, 2023). *Circular No. A-94, Guidelines and Discount Rates for Benefit-Cost Analysis of Federal Programs*. Washington, DC: Executive Office of the President.

PMI (2021). *A Guide to the Project Management Body of Knowledge (PMBOK), Seventh Edition*. Newtown Square: Project Management Institute.

Sunstein, C. (2000). Cognition and Cost-Benefit Analysis. *The Journal of Legal Studies*, 29(S2): 1059–1103.

The White House (1993). Executive Order 12866: Regulatory Planning and Review. *Federal Register*, 58(190).

United States Environmental Protection Agency (2000). *Guidelines for Preparing Economic Analysis*. Washington, DC: Office of the Administrator.

United States Office of Management and Budget (January 11, 1996). *Economic Analysis of Federal Regulations Under Executive Order 12866*. Washington, DC: Executive Office of the President.

Yates, B.T. (2021). Toward Collaborative Cost-Inclusive Evaluation: Adaptations and Transformations for Evaluators and Economists. *Evaluation and Program Planning*, 89.

Yates, B.T. and Persaud, N. (2023). *Cost-Inclusive Evaluation: Planning It, Doing It, Using It*. New York: The Guilford Press.

Zwikael, O. and Huemann, M. (2023). Project Benefits Management: Making an Impact on Organizations and Society Through Projects and Programs. *International Journal of Project Management*, 41(8).

6

QUALITATIVE CONCEPTS

Intangible costs and benefits tend to be irreducible; it is difficult to assign them a value, but publicly funded projects may require the quantification of various non-commercial benefits, equating them to financial values for ease of mathematical calculation. If two alternatives are found through quantitative analysis to be economically equivalent, qualitative elements may be used as a tiebreaker to help select the best scenario.

For many public projects and public policymaking, a traditional economic analysis is too restrictive. Various methods exist to consider qualitative elements in a strategic analysis without resorting to monetization. These methods enable the analyst to include non-quantitative information in the analysis, ensuring visibility and consideration of elements that require more description and nuance, which would otherwise be omitted or potentially mis-quantified in a purely quantitative analysis. Several of these approaches, varying in levels of sophistication, are discussed below. None of these qualitative multi-criteria analysis (MCA) methods are a stand-alone substitution for quantitative analysis; rather, they are tools intended to be used in combination with each other and with quantitative methods.

It is worth noting that, when the analysis contains several qualitative criteria against which scenarios are measured, it is unlikely any scenario will be ranked the highest for all the qualitative criteria. It is more likely that different qualitative criteria will favor different scenarios. As such, multi-criteria methods of analysis require compromise and the ranking of criteria.

Benefits other than cost are usually not considered in economic analysis, or may be mentioned in passing but not analyzed. They may

DOI: 10.4324/9781003014928-7

be analyzed and reported separately from the cost analysis. Whether this is due to a lack of available funding for expanded analysis, the finance professional's discomfort with non-quantitative concepts, or some ingrained negative perception of benefits as a "socialist" concept is difficult to determine.

This book advocates for the inclusion of qualitative elements in project analysis because non-revenue benefits and societal value are becoming increasingly important to businesses under the twin umbrellas of sustainability and resilience. Requests for analysis of such benefits are only going to increase, at client request.

PROS AND CONS LIST

The simplest analytical method is a pros and cons list. In this approach, pros (benefits) and cons (disbenefits) are listed in separate columns, at which point the table is reviewed and a decision is made based on the strongest pros and weakest cons. Line items may include quantitative elements or calculations, but there will usually be significantly more qualitative line items than quantitative. This method requires little time and effort, apart from some brainstorming and introspection. It is useful for simple situations, often yes/no scenarios, and the analysis is subjective.

In the example below, a pros and cons list was created for each of the four washing machine scenarios. During the analysis, two of the scenarios failed to meet minimum performance criteria, were determined to be unacceptable, and were thus eliminated. Quantitative calculations were simple because they were all expected to occur within the same limited time period. Unexpectedly, the final decision was primarily economic, not subjective, based on the initial cost to purchase or repair and the relative cost of potential future repairs. Had the "upgrade" option been viable, the outcome of the analysis may well have been different (requiring a decision matrix, discussed next).

DECISION MATRIX

Similar to a pros and cons list, a decision matrix (also called a Pugh matrix or criteria rating form) can be used to compare both quantitative and qualitative elements that are subject to the same assessment

Table 6.1 Pros and cons list

Repair		*Replace - Equivalent*		*Replace - Upgrade*		*Discard*	
Pro	*Con*	*Pro*	*Con*	*Pro*	*Con*	*Pro*	*Con*
Familiarity	$800	$600	Basic features	Smartphone app	$1,700	$50	Wash by hand
Small agitator	No new features	Dials only/ easier repairs	Large agitator	No agitator	Unfamiliar	Could retrofit area for dog wash	Laundromat inconvenient
See-through lid	Too deep	Less deep	Not stackable	Pet Pro option, steam/allergen/ silk/wool cycles	May leak		Dry cleaning cost
Fits in space available	Digital controls/ costly repairs Not stackable	Fits in space available	Metal lid	Front load	Deep footprint		
Ranked: #2		**Ranked: #1**		**Doesn't fit in space available**		**Unacceptable**	

criteria. The difference between a decision matrix and a pros and cons list is that a decision matrix includes scoring, whereas a pros and cons list does not. Significant qualitative elements (known as considerations) are ranked using an ordinal scale (such as one to five, where five is the highest), and weighting may also be added. The number of considerations is typically limited to a maximum of ten. Both rankings and weightings are subjective and may be controversial. A decision matrix is used when the considerations have different levels of importance to the project. It is easy to construct and conveys the decision-making process in a simple, easy-to-understand table.

Weighting

Weighting is used to reflect the relative importance of the qualitative or quantitative elements, as agreed by stakeholder decision-makers. As applied below in Table 6.2, weighting assigned to the cost element of the scenario analysis below indicates that cost is considered an important factor in the washing machine selection process. Multiplying the cost score by two effectively skews the analysis results toward a decision that is influenced by the cost of each option.

In evaluation and policy development, weighting is used to create distributional equity of benefits and maximize social welfare in scenario selection. An unweighted analysis is ignorant of benefits (and disbenefits) that disproportionately affect certain segments of society. Stakeholder identification and standing, as discussed in Chapter 3 of this book, are key to the weighting process. Weighting is then used in the analysis to reflect the relative importance of social welfare elements, and offset disproportional effects.

As mentioned above, the use of weighting in policymaking and societal initiatives can be controversial. When weighting is applied in an analysis, a second analysis (essentially a sensitivity test) should be conducted without weighting to understand its effect on the analysis outcome. The justification and methodology for weighting, if applied, should be described and documented.

Returning to the washing machine example (omitting the unacceptable option) and using a scoring scale of zero to one (where one is the best and highest score), the decision matrix looks like this[1]:

Table 6.2 Decision matrix with weighting

Options	*Cost*	*Weighted cost (x2)*	*Repair cost*	*Additional features*	*Depth*	*Agitator type*	*Learning curve*	*Score*
Repair	$800–0.5	1	High - 0	No - 0	High - 0	Low profile - 0.5	No - 1	**2.5**
Replace with equivalent	$600–1	2	Low - 1	No - 0	Low - 0.5	Standard - 0	Some - 0.5	**4**
Upgrade	$1,700–0	0	High - 0	Yes - 1	Front load - 1	None - 1	Yes - 0	**3**

Note that, in this decision matrix, the quantified cost is translated to a scoring scale and then weighted for the purposes of analysis.

Another form of analysis, lexicographic ordering, uses the same criteria as the decision matrix, except in an iterative fashion. Scenarios are ranked according to the most important criterion, and any scenarios tied for the top score are then ranked again, this time according to the second most important criterion. The analysis continues in this fashion until only one scenario remains. The concept of "importance" is, of course, subjective. When there are a large number of scenarios to be considered, lexicographic ordering is a quick way to reduce the population to a handful for further analysis.

COST-EFFECTIVENESS ANALYSIS

Cost-effectiveness analysis (CEA) divides the present value of summed costs (C) by an effect measure (E). This is one of the two most common calculations in public project and evaluation, the other being the benefit-cost ratio, discussed in Chapter 5 of this book. It can be used to compare scenarios when the expected type of benefits from the scenarios are the same.

$$Cost\ Effectiveness = \frac{C}{E}$$

Equation 6.1 Cost effectiveness ratio

It is worth noting that cost-effectiveness is not synonymous with cost savings. The cost-effectiveness (also known as least-cost) approach is one that focuses on optimization in the use of funds and is thus prevalent in government analyses for comparing scenarios with the same measurable objective. Note that CEA is used for only one outcome at a time and, should the scenario have multiple objectives, the calculation would need to be reperformed for each objective. The denominator (effectiveness) is a quantitative measure of some desired benefit, outcome, or output, often a potential long-term government policy outcome or improvement, using a numeric scale (such as 0 to 100, where 100 is the highest).

As with traditional economic analysis, one of the options considered is that of the status quo, or the current standard of care, used as a control group when calculating cost-effectiveness. Cost-effectiveness analysis is often used to evaluate projects that have already been implemented where actual outcomes are measurable, but it can also be used to compare scenarios where planned outcomes are quantifiable. For planned scenarios, the outcome measures may be used later as metrics for performance monitoring and management.

The CEA result may be compared against the CEA for other projects with the same objective, or may be compared against a benchmark or goal. The outcome measurement may be based on external studies and probabilities, and may be highly subjective; many measures are difficult to quantify. Examples of outcomes include regional development, societal cohesion, improved accessibility, number of participants, and other socioeconomic impacts.

Cost-utility analysis

In the health sector, a similar approach to CEA is known as cost-utility analysis (CUA), which divides the present value of summed costs (C) by an utility measure (U) multiplied by the probability of the effect occurring (p). A frequently used utility measure in healthcare scenarios is quality-adjusted life years (QALYs). The probability times utility measure is known as the expected utility.

$$Cost\,Utility\,Ratio = \frac{C}{p \times U}$$

Equation 6.2 Cost utility ratio

As with CEA, the outcome measurement may be based on external studies and probabilities, and may be highly subjective; many measures are difficult to quantify.

Cost-consequence analysis

Cost-consequence analysis (CCA) is a quantitative method that considers both costs and beneficial outcomes but reports them in a descriptive table instead of summing all quantifiable outcomes. This disaggregated and transparent approach provides greater insight to the analysis approach. CCA is useful for scenarios that have multiple planned outcomes, enabling comparison across all cost and non-cost outcomes with an appropriate level of detail such that attention is drawn equally to each outcome. This type of analysis is often used for healthcare scenarios.

Because the outcomes might not be equivalent in purpose (e.g., clinical outcomes are not the same as carbon-neutral outcomes), CCA enables the use of different denominators (effect measures) that are fit for purpose per outcome. This is different from CEA and CUA approaches; as discussed above, CEA uses a unidimensional measure of effectiveness and CUA uses a single outcome measure such as QALYs. Because different units are used within the analysis, there is no treatment (weighting) of different outcomes to indicate their relative importance.

MAXIMIN ANALYSIS

A maximin analysis takes a pessimistic approach to decision-making, and is widely used in game theory. The methodology considers known uncertainties and risks and identifies the worst possible outcome for each scenario. The scenarios are rank ordered, and the "least worst" scenario selected, thus taking a conservative stance. There are two other approaches: maximax analysis takes a highly optimistic view and selects the best-case scenario with the highest return inclusive of risk, and minimax (or minimax regret) seeks to minimize the maximum possible loss (and thus regret).

Criteria for each scenario are assigned expected values and then compared. These criteria may be quantitative or qualitative, and are usually scored on a scale of one to ten where ten is the highest. For example, pessimistic outcomes (criteria) could be the number of deaths or accidents, level of pollution or contamination, or carbon load. In a simplified version of the trolley problem, the preferred "least worst" utilitarian scenario is the instance where only one person is killed, if all lives are considered equal.

Returning to the washing machine example (omitting the unacceptable option) and using a scoring scale of zero-to-five (where five is the highest), the maximin matrix returns this result:

Again, in this maximin matrix, the quantified cost is translated to a scoring scale for the purposes of analysis.

Table 6.3 Maximin matrix

Options	*Cost*	*Repair cost*	*Additional features*	*Depth*	*Agitator type*	*Learning curve*	*Score*
Repair	4	5	1	1	1	5	**17**
Replace with equivalent	5	5	2	1	1	3	**17**
Upgrade	1	3	5	5	5	1	**20**

Note that a scale of one-to-five was used instead of the recommended scale of zero-to-ten to avoid the "hidden importance multiplier" effect of the zero-to-ten scale; where there is not much intermediate scoring, meaning the highest and lowest scale values are most often used, the zero-to-ten scale behaves as weighting without being explicitly stated as such. Because there is no additional weighting of the columns (as was done in the decision matrix example), the highest-scoring scenario differs from previous analyses.

OBJECTIVES-BASED IMPACT EVALUATION

Impact evaluation (IE) considers the effect that a scenario (often called an intervention) is having or has had on a given population or entity, often as part of a continuous monitoring program with the intent of adjusting the intervention in some fashion to better meet stated objectives and definitions of success. Adjustments may mean terminating the intervention, implementing changes, scaling up a pilot program, or effecting improvements to a future intervention.

Also used in business analysis, IE studies benefits and costs (termed positive and negative effects) using a MCA approach. The difference between IE and economic analysis is that IE includes in the analysis both direct and indirect primary and secondary effects, whether intended or unintended, and the analysis often takes a very long-term view. Standard criteria for IE may be ranked using a purpose-developed rubric that addresses such criteria as relevance, effectiveness, efficiency, impact, and sustainability. Other commonly used benchmarks and indices for development projects are socioeconomic in nature, such as quality of life, equity, and human rights. Socioeconomic impact analysis (IA) is a specialized type of objectives-based IE that focuses on socio-cultural and economic impacts such as health and well-being, individual and family-level impacts, the protection of cultural, historical, sacred, and archaeological resources, land use and environmental effects, business and employment opportunities, availability of social services and infrastructure, population and cost of living changes, changes in political and societal structures, innovation and knowledge creation, and more. Selected criteria are obtained from the documented theory of change for the intervention, in which an influence diagram explicitly maps the relationship between the intervention (scenario or policy) and expected outcomes.

The simplest outputs from an IA are checklists, goal achievement matrices, and performance reports; more detailed outputs combine economic analysis with qualitative and multi-criteria methods. IA may involve controlled trials or other types of experimental design. It might not always be possible to conduct a thorough IE, owing to lack of data, timing, and determinations of causality.

The qualitative methods discussed above are merely a fraction of the many different approaches that can be applied in strategic project analysis. The choice of approach depends on the available data components of the problem and scenarios being analyzed, resources (time, cost) allocated for performing the strategic project analysis, and the analysis objectives. It is not unusual for several approaches to be used and the results compared.

VALUE FOR MONEY

Value for money (VFM or VfM) is a measure of benefit that applies the three fundamental concepts of performance audit: economy, efficiency, and effectiveness, and may include equity and sustainability. When used in a culture of continuous improvement, the optimization and maximization of these concepts can improve organizational maturity[2]. In this context, economy is related to the minimization of resource use (low cost) while meeting minimum requirements, efficiency focuses on the optimal use of the same resources (low waste) with a goal of scalability, and effectiveness (E) is a measure of success against a stated outcome.

Equity implies concessions to correct resource imbalances according to need, and sustainability considers impacts (often environmental) on future generations. VFM is not about merely minimizing cost.

The metrics used for VFM are specific to the objectives of the analysis and the phase of the project. Metrics may be monetary, quantitative, or qualitative (non-monetized). Development of metrics and scoring may require benchmarking against peer programs, or may be related to target outcomes. All specified fundamental elements must be considered for the VFM analysis to be complete and the elements may be weighted according to relative importance.

In the VFM scenario shown in Table 6.4 and Figure 6.1, value is scored against a range of one (1) to ten (10) and cost is stated in thousands (K). If a maximum cost threshold was established at $8 million and a minimum value score was established at five (5), only scenarios three (3), nine (9), and ten (10) would be viable.

Unlike some of the other strategic project analysis concepts discussed herein, VFM is both an ex-ante tool for decision-making and an iterative process that specifies economic analysis and supplemental reviews be undertaken at specific points in time (often percentage complete, as quartiles), or milestones. It incorporates elements of value engineering, risk management, life-cycle cost, stakeholder management, and quantitative analysis with tools for good governance (such as formal policies, compliance with laws and requirements, and control procedures) and reporting. Milestones may be established in conjunction with project stage gates or the funding lifecycle, or an annual VFM assessment may be required.

Table 6.4 Cost vs. value

Scenario #	*Value*	*Cost ($K)*
Scenario 1	4	4,381
Scenario 2	7	8,104
Scenario 3	9	4,058
Scenario 4	4	9,319
Scenario 5	2	5,560
Scenario 6	3	9,819
Scenario 7	5	5,344
Scenario 8	5	7,795
Scenario 9	8	6,123
Scenario 10	9	5,318

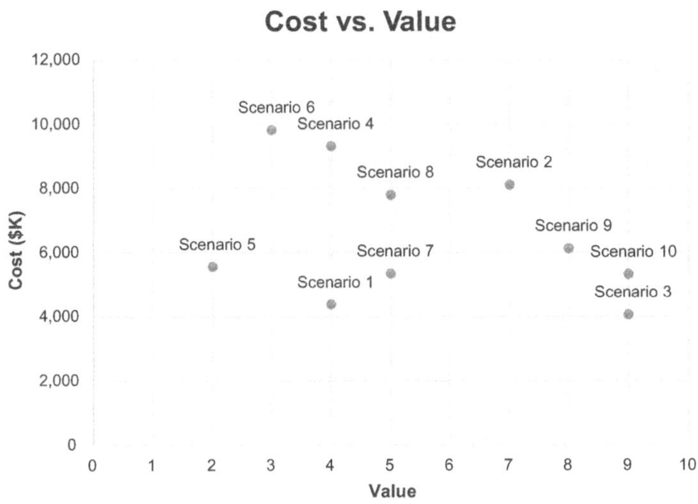

Figure 6.1 Cost vs. value

Quantitative methods may be utilized in the VFM process. Non-quantitative methods described above may also be included, or a wish list of benefits may be weighted and assessed using a checklist. VFM is a true multi-criteria analysis approach to strategic project analysis, embracing both interdisciplinary and multi-sectoral methods. VFM is often applied to development projects and public-private partnerships.

TRIPLE BOTTOM LINE COST BENEFIT ANALYSIS

Triple Bottom Line Cost Benefit Analysis (TBL-CBA) blends traditional CBA with lifecycle cost analysis and also adds societal and environmental criteria, using monetary proxy values for those effects. It is increasingly being used for public sector construction projects, with the addition of societal and environmental criteria reflecting growing stakeholder interest in those benefits. This approach to CBA may be required by funding agencies or be a prerequisite for specialty certifications.

Examples of societal and environmental effects considered in a TBL-CBA include reduction of carbon emissions, reduction of air pollution, reduction of heat island impacts, improvements to water quality, reduction of flooding, and increases in property value. The effects are correlated with engineering design and materials used. For infrastructure projects, the TBL-CBA scope may include operations and maintenance and an extended timeframe of analysis, as the expectation is that societal and environmental benefits will continue to accrue and multiply over the lifetime of a scenario. TBL-CBA analysis is used to inform design improvements in combination with value engineering. As attention to TBL-CBA grows, so will realizations about the pitfalls of monetary proxy values and attention to the use of additional multi-criteria and qualitative elements.

SOCIAL RETURN ON INVESTMENT

Social return on investment (SROI) is a triple-bottom-line approach to forecasting or retrospectively measuring societal, economic, and environmental impacts. It is a quantitative approach that monetizes benefits and disbenefits using financial proxies, to calculate a societal-value-to-investment ratio. The calculation is similar to that used for benefit cost ratio, discussed in Chapter 5 of this book. SROI blends all the concepts and processes of CBA with IE skills to calculate societal value for money.

Key to the methodology are stakeholder involvement and the selection of information based on materiality. It also introduces several counterfactuals, which are essentially treated as disbenefits:

- Deadweight: outcomes that would occur regardless of the scenario, stated as an amount or a percentage
- Displacement: benefits that result in an expense to others or offset another outcome, stated as an amount or a percentage and sometimes completely offsetting another outcome for a net benefit of zero
- Drop-off: the period in which benefits stop accruing to a portion of stakeholders, shown as a percentage deduction per year
- Attribution: third-party contributions to outcomes, often calculated as a percentage of the outcome

The SROI ratio is calculated using the following equation:

$$SROI = \frac{Net\ Value\ Created}{Value\ of\ Investment}$$

Equation 6.3 Social return on investment

PROBLEMS, REFLECTIONS, AND EXERCISES

1. How might qualitative analysis methods be useful to you in real life? Provide two (2) examples.
2. Explain why a decision matrix might be used for scenario selection instead of a pros and cons list. Provide an example.
3. Find one published example each of a cost-effectiveness analysis, an objectives-based IE, and a value-for-money study. Cite your sources.
4. How might qualitative analysis be used to supplement the results obtained from an economic analysis? Provide an example, and explain how this might affect decision-making.
5. Explain in your own words why the use of an effectiveness measure or utility measure can be potentially problematic.
6. Explain in your own words how weighting might unfairly affect scenario selection.

NOTES

1 Just for fun, the analysis above includes the (physically impossible) option of upgrading to a better washing machine. The author is simultaneously relieved and disappointed to note the upgrade did not achieve the high score.

2 Nalewaik, A. and Mills, A. (2016). Project Performance Review: Capturing the Value of Audit, Oversight, and Compliance for Project Success, p. 41–42. Abingdon-on-Thames: Routledge.

BIBLIOGRAPHY

Acland, D. and Greenberg, D.H. (2023). Distributional Weighting and Welfare/Equity Tradeoffs: A New Approach. *Journal of Benefit-Cost Analysis*, 14(1): 68–92.

Campen, J.T. (1986). *Benefit, Cost, and Beyond: The Political Economy of Benefit-Cost Analysis*, p. 52. Cambridge MA: Ballinger.

Griniece, E. et al. (2020). *The Guidebook for Socio-Economic Impact Assessment of Research Infrastructures.* Brussels: Research Infrastructure Impact Assessment paTHwayS (RI PATHS) Consortium.

Lohmann, R.A. (2020). Break Even Analysis: A Tool for Budget Planning. *Faculty & Staff Scholarship*: 2585. https://researchrepository.wvu.edu/faculty_publications/2585.

RICS (2020). *Measuring Social Value in Infrastructure Projects: Insights from the Public Sector*. London: The Royal Institution of Chartered Surveyors.

Sunstein, C., (2000). Cognition and Cost-Benefit Analysis. *The Journal of Legal Studies*, 29(S2): 1059–1103.

The SROI Network (2012). *A Guide to Social Return on Investment*. Liverpool: Social Value UK.

Yates, B.T. and Persaud, N. (2023). *Cost-Inclusive Evaluation: Planning It, Doing It, Using It*. New York: The Guilford Press.

7

PERSPECTIVE, BIAS, AND ETHICS

PERSPECTIVE

Perspective is a point of view, a way of looking at a problem. The outcome of any strategic project analysis is wholly dependent on its perspective; the outcome of the analysis may well change if a different legitimate perspective is considered. Looking back to the list of stakeholders in Chapter 3 of this book, there may be many potential perspectives for the analysis.

There are three common perspectives in cost-benefit analysis. Market perspective takes a purely financial approach, focusing on market prices of costs and benefits. Investor perspective focuses on maximizing profit. Societal perspective considers costs and benefits from a socio-economic angle, applying shadow pricing for qualitative elements.

The perspective (analysis lens) problem is particularly true of the political applications of cost-benefit analysis, wherein multiple agencies compete vigorously for government funding and policymaking is subject to powerful influence by bureaucrats, lobbying, and special interest groups. For example, a toll road project analysis will yield different results from the perspective of the for-profit private operator and the public agency serving an infrastructure need. For policy and government funding applications the analysis report needs to clearly specify and justify the perspective taken, stating whether the selected perspective is that of spenders (those who are delivering necessary services) or guardians (the funding agency). Ideally, a thorough process would provide two analyses, one from each perspective.

Perspective may also differ depending on who is performing the analysis. The analysis may be performed by organization employees

DOI: 10.4324/9781003014928-8

or by external consultants. Internal staff tend to be overly optimistic and may be influenced by management to favor a particular scenario or analysis outcome. On the other hand, internal staff have easier access to organizational information, past projects, and knowledge of culture, and the analysis will be less expensive to perform. External consultants may be less likely than internal staff to have incentive to distort data, have the ability to practice both divergent (creative, nonlinear) and convergent (structured, logical) thinking, and (assuming a rigorous selection process) will likely have more experience in similar types of analysis. External consultants might not always be independent, and their loyalties and duties must be well understood by the analysts. Because analyst independence is key to unbiased perspective, it is generally recommended that external independent consultants conduct the analysis to try to ensure impartiality, necessary skepticism, freedom from influence, critical thinking, and objectivity. That said, a truly independent perspective may be difficult to achieve.

Selecting a consultant

The consultant selection process can help ensure independence and neutrality, and improve the quality of services. Although the client typically has little control over the actions of the consultant (such as productivity, level of diligence, and integrity) during the consulting process, the procurement process and contract can be utilized to influence both behavior and outcome. In-person interviews, team member resumes, sample reports, and reference checks can be helpful in evaluating consultant proposals and team composition, and contract language can prevent team member bait-and-switch (or understaffing) and ensure better transparency of the consulting process by requiring interim progress reports.

BIAS

In the context of strategic decision-making, bias can be described as conscious or subconscious prejudice in favor of or against a scenario, which may result in a lack of objectivity and illogical or irrational choices. In general, strong governance and decision-making frameworks can be used to help prevent bias, along with independent analysis, seeking disconfirming evidence, and practicing critical questioning. That said, an analysis completely free from bias may be difficult to achieve.

There are over 150 types of cognitive bias, some of which are particularly pervasive in strategic decision-making. Several of these are described below.

Action bias

Action bias is a tendency to choose a scenario that is different from the status quo, owing to a sense of needing to take action, even if there is greater risk or ambiguity. It may result in impulsive choices; action bias often occurs during an emergency, providing the organization with a sense of control during a dire situation.

Drivers' reactions to a traffic jam are good examples of action bias. Some drivers will change lanes to try to gain an advantage instead of sitting still in traffic and waiting for it to clear. Others will choose to exit a highway and take surface streets in the hope that the new route, even if longer in distance, might be shorter in time than staying on the congested highway. Instinctively, the driver prefers to be moving and doing something, rather than staying put and seemingly doing nothing.

A robust and formal decision-making process can help prevent action bias.

Anchoring

Anchoring bias is a subconscious inclination to fixate on data already received, sometimes to the point of ignoring new information.

Anchoring can often be seen in project planning and budgeting, affecting scheduling, estimating, and value judgment by focusing unnecessarily on an early "ballpark" (or "back of napkin") quantification or guesstimate. It may be used as a sales technique, in which an initial price is established as an unconscious baseline.

Anchoring is very difficult to overcome. A remedy for anchoring is re-anchoring, which means challenging the anchor point and effectively replacing it with a new benchmark based on relevant and accurate data. This requires recognizing and acknowledging that the anchor exists.

Attentional bias

Attentional bias is a tendency to focus disproportionately on certain elements of a scenario or specific types of information while at the same time ignoring other elements. Attentional bias is closely related to risk tolerance and results in skewed perception and incomplete analysis.

Feature positive effect is a form of attentional bias that focuses heavily on positive outcomes. It may occur when an analysis is conducted with limited resources or time, or may be the result of a herding (conformity) effect. Catastrophic thinking is a form of attentional bias that focuses heavily on negative outcomes.

Attentional bias may occur in strategic project analysis when efforts are directed toward scenarios and elements that are easy to analyze and quantify instead of considering all possible costs, benefits, and disbenefits. Other examples of attentional bias include racial profiling, adherence to religious and political ideologies, and gender discrimination.

Bandwagon effect

The bandwagon effect is a phenomenon that occurs when individuals begin to show preference for scenarios that are favored by others, possibly driven by pressure to conform. The bandwagon effect may result in the rejection of less popular but still viable scenarios.

It is a form of groupthink and conformity bias that is common in politics and investing, and is amplified by visibility. For example, aggressive marketing may cause a consumer to believe "everyone" is buying a particular product, prompting that consumer to do the same.

The bandwagon effect may be overcome by actively seeking out contradictory information, creating a safe space where dissenting opinions are allowed, identifying buzzwords, and encouraging critical thinking and diversity of perspectives.

Commitment bias

Commitment bias occurs when an entity continues to invest resources in a project despite new information indicating that investment is unwise. The sunk cost fallacy, in which an organization refuses to abandon a failing project, is an example of commitment bias; in public infrastructure, there aren't very many half-built dams or highways to nowhere.

The remedy for commitment bias requires a robust project review process, truthfulness in project reporting, a willingness to change one's mind, and a renewed focus on strategic goals and metrics. Once commitment bias has occurred, a change in leadership may be required for an organization to alter course.

Confirmation bias

Confirmation bias is a tendency to select only data that reaffirms past decisions or supports a theory or preference, rejecting other available contradictory information. Confirmation bias results in an incomplete analysis. Confirmation bias may result in missed opportunities, owing to the rejection of otherwise viable scenarios.

The author's personal example comes from long-distance swimming. On a Catalina Channel solo swim, one of the engines on the twin-engine support boat failed, producing a knocking sound. On a subsequent English Channel solo swim, she heard a clanking sound and promptly assumed it was coming from the support boat's engine. It turned out the sound was caused by her teeth chattering from hypothermia, which she discovered much later.

Confirmation bias may be overcome by ensuring neutrality in data analyzed, actively seeking out contradictory information, embracing a willingness to change one's mind, creating a safe space where dissenting opinions are allowed, and encouraging critical thinking and diversity of perspectives.

Endowment effect

The endowment effect is the quantitative gap between willingness to pay and willingness to accept. It is a type of loss aversion that is closely tied to sales and marketing. It also reflects esteem value, which is higher than book or market value, owing to subjective attribution.

The endowment effect can be seen in action in real estate listing prices and used vehicle prices.

The remedy for the endowment effect in cost-benefit analysis is the use of market value.

Expedience bias

Expedience bias occurs when the analysis has been rushed, owing to pressure to make a decision quickly, resulting in conclusions drawn from incomplete data. It is similar to action bias.

A robust and formal decision-making process can help prevent expedience bias.

Experience bias

Experience bias occurs when the analyst or organization allows past experience and preferred methods to influence their decision-making instead of allowing the data to guide their conclusions. Experience bias hinders problem-solving and creativity, and is similar to confirmation bias.

For example, an analyst may adhere to familiar (and thus seemingly easier) methods of analysis and quantification instead of trying a new, more appropriate technique to solve a problem (or evaluate a scenario).

Overcoming experience bias requires recognizing and acknowledging that the bias exists, exploring alternative approaches, and reaffirming hard data as the authentic driver in analysis.

Framing effect

Framing effect is a type of misrepresentation in which information is presented with the intent to influence the selection of a scenario. Framing bias may occur in weighting, the analysis report, or presentation to decision-makers, and is a significant influence on public opinion.

Narrative fallacy is a type of storytelling that is related to framing bias. It affects decision-making when the appeal of the story, or conclusions drawn from the story, overshadows objective conclusions drawn from facts and analysis.

Almost all marketing presents information or products to a consumer audience using framing effects. Consider advertising, product location in a store or on a shelf, and product placement in films and television. The framing effect is also readily apparent in legal proceedings, as each lawyer pleads their case.

A remedy for framing bias requires reframing the presentation to ensure equal focus on positive and negative outcomes and clear, reproducible justification for decisions made.

Immediate gratification bias

Immediate gratification (also known as instant gratification) bias is the human tendency to select immediate rewards instead of future rewards (delayed gratification), even if the future option value exceeds that of the present option value. The reward may be something physical such as a purchase or activity, or conceptual such as an opportunity. Immediate gratification bias is well described by the popular saying, "A bird in the hand is worth two in the bush."

In strategic project analysis, immediate gratification bias is known as hyperbolic or temporal discounting, in which the analysis favors short-term rewards over long-term rewards even if the short-term rewards are smaller. High discount rates used in cost-benefit analysis encourage immediate gratification bias by discounting long-term rewards to the point of being negligible.

Clearly defined strategic long-term objectives can help overcome immediate gratification bias.

Overconfidence bias

Overconfidence bias results in overly optimistic forecasts of scenario elements, and is prevalent in leadership and project management. The opposite of overconfidence or optimism bias is the prudence trap.

The planning fallacy, in which task time is underestimated, is related to overconfidence bias as applied to schedule. The Dunning-Kruger effect is a form of overconfidence bias as applied to competence.

Decision-making in government policy and major investment is fraught with competition for funds and, thus, the need to create a compelling and winning argument for selection. This pressure may influence analysts to make deliberate edits to the analysis, obscuring value assignments and costing, and skewing results toward the optimistic. Strategic misrepresentation is a conscious version of optimism bias in which costs and disbenefits are understated, forecasts are buoyant, and benefits and return on investment are overstated to ensure project approval and funding.

Overcoming overconfidence bias requires recognizing and acknowledging that the bias exists, considering a different perspective, and reaffirming hard data as the authentic driver in analysis.

Pro-innovation bias

Pro-innovation bias occurs when new technology or concepts are preferred over tried and true solutions, regardless of increased risk. It may present itself as weighting or high benefits values. Pro-innovation bias is a form of overconfidence (optimism) bias that may result in an incomplete analysis by excluding other viable scenarios.

Sponsorship bias

Sponsorship bias describes a situation in which the analysis is impacted by the objectives of the entity funding the analysis. This is an extreme example of investor perspective, which is pervasive in project analysis, especially for public sector projects and policymaking.

A study of 2,437 medical cost-effectiveness analyses concluded that analyses sponsored by industry were more likely to report a high cost-effectiveness ratio.[1]

Perspective and bias are closely related. For example, cost-benefit analyses performed for investment by a private company will take an investor perspective, focusing on maximum profit and the company's best interests. This impartiality presents not just as perspective but also as sponsorship bias.

Status quo bias

Status quo bias is the tendency to prefer taking no action, representing a comfort level with the way things are and an aversion to risk and change. Status quo bias results in obstacles to innovation. Action bias is the opposite of status quo bias.

An example of status quo bias is the tendency to keep ordering the same meal at a restaurant because it is familiar (and, presumably, well-liked) instead of trying a different item on the menu.

Overcoming status quo bias requires enforcing the obligation to explore alternative scenarios, and reaffirming hard data as the authentic driver in analysis.

Although specific remedies are listed above for each type of bias, there are some general steps that may be taken to minimize these and other types of bias. Avoiding bias, and thus improving decision-making, may be achieved by:

- Engaging in more thorough inspection and analysis
- Gathering more data
- Comparing the consequences of potential actions
- Envisioning the worst-case scenario
- Seeking alternate and diverse perspectives
- Reinforcing objectivity
- Removing emotions from the discussion
- Encouraging a "growth and change" mindset
- Practicing mindfulness
- Applying critical thinking and critical questioning

ETHICS

Every situation or decision has an ethical dimension. It is essential in cost-benefit analysis, especially when considering societal benefits. It is easy enough to say one should always do the right thing, but that often becomes difficult in an organizational context where the analyst reports to upper management and/or clients. "Blind, unquestioning obedience and loyalty do not enable ethical decision-making"[2].

Indeed, various government guidelines for strategic project analysis specify the honesty and integrity of the analyst as requirements[3]. It is well-recognized that the action of determining stakeholders' standing is an ethical question, and trade-offs between scenarios may even pose an ethical dilemma in which unpleasant choices and complex judgments are made. All the steps in the strategic project analysis process have an ethical component, including scope definition (and limitation), the identification (or exclusion) of legitimate scenarios, subjectivity and comprehensiveness in quantification and valuation, subjectivity in ranking, and influences in scenario selection. Critics of cost benefit analysis believe it to be fraught with ethics concerns.

There are many different "schools" of ethics. One that applies well to cost-benefit analysis is known as consequence-based ethics[4], defined as doing that which produces the greatest good. Consequence-based ethics require a forecast of the results of actions taken, much as a strategic project analysis attempts to forecast the costs and benefits of a scenario. In the modern world, "greater good" concepts have broadened to include impacts on society, sustainability, and the natural environment - the United Nations Sustainable Development Goals (SDG) have the concept of greater good at their very core, with the aim of solving persistent wicked problems. Here too, deontological ethics[5] and Aristotle's "Nicomachean Ethics" concepts of teleology or consequentialism are relevant: justice, fairness, prudence (phronesis), the improvement of lives, and well-being (eudaimonia).

Members of professional institutions are typically bound by an ethics code, which can serve as a guideline for behavior. Concepts of honesty, integrity, professional responsibility, and independence/objectivity are specifically mentioned. Central to such ethics codes is the avoidance of deception, which may occur in false or misleading statements, omissions, and half-truths. In the author's experience, however, such codes are generally ignored and rarely enforced.

Documentation of the cost-benefit analysis effort, referenced earlier as a good practice, serves several purposes. The primary objective is to create a record, capturing calculations, exclusions, context, and intent, both to answer future questions about the analysis and create an auditable historical record. However, such documentation also serves to satisfy the ethical component of the analysis, satisfying goals of clear communication, accountability, confidence, assurance, rigor, and transparency by capturing comprehensive and substantiated information. It can be said that proper documentation is a mechanism for ethics. To be truly ethical, documentation should also include a discussion of any controversial assumptions and their impact on the outcome of the analysis.

It is entirely possible for a scenario to be selected where costs exceed benefits, especially when qualitative elements are considered to be significant but are not included in the quantitative calculations, and/or societal benefits are expected to occur well beyond the timeframe (scope) of the analysis. It may be argued that this is an example of ethical decision-making, choosing the option that is morally right[6]. It goes without saying that this doesn't happen very often in the real world without a large dollop of altruism and generous donors. More often, utilitarian principles are followed with the goal of achieving improvements for the greatest number of people (consider the trolley problem, a thought experiment in which one life is weighed against five others). Efficiency in the use of funds is the normative criterion.

Public price-based cost-benefit analyses and the public policies based thereon readily lend themselves to the unethical. At best, these analyses are imprecise by design (and scope), yet through their pseudo-scientific and quantitative presentation they falsely convey a high level of confidence. Compounding the problem, they try to express in black and white that which exists in shades of grey, and quantify the unquantifiable. At worst, both the analyses and any resulting public policies are subject to problems of lobbying, opportunism, political influence, self-interest, bias, and perspective. No amount of rigorous methodology is an adequate substitute for ethical judgment.

REFLECTIONS AND EXERCISES

1. Find five (5) published examples of cost-benefit analysis, and identify the perspective used for each. Cite your sources.
2. Is there a difference in perspective between engineering economics and welfare economics? Explain.
3. Identify five (5) types of cognitive bias that you recognize in yourself. The list of biases need not be restricted to those identified in the text above.
4. Are you bound by an ethics code? Consider all possible sources, including your employer, religion, culture, and any organizations of which you are a member. Explain.
5. If you are subject to several ethics codes, consider the differences between them. Do the ethics codes conflict in any way? Explain and discuss.
6. Describe a situation in which a scenario might be selected even though costs exceed benefits.
7. Explain in your own words how lobbying and political influence might affect the outcome of an analysis.

NOTES

1 Xie, F. and Zhou, T. (2022). Industry Sponsorship Bias in Cost-Effectiveness Analysis: Registry-Based Analysis. *The BMJ*, 377: e069573.
2 Ashrafi, R. (2003). *Ethics in Project Management.* Fall 2003: 6–7.

3 United States Environmental Protection Agency (2000). *Guidelines for Preparing Economic Analysis*. Washington DC: Office of the Administrator and United States Office of Management and Budget (January 11, 1996). *Economic Analysis of Federal Regulations Under Executive Order 12866*. Washington, DC: Executive Office of the President.
4 Mill, J.S. (1806–73)
5 Kant, I. (1724–1804)
6 Economics was originally a branch of moral philosophy. Smith, A. (1776), reprint by The Library of Economics and Liberty (2018). *An Inquiry into the Nature and Causes of the Wealth of Nations*. Carmel, IN: Econlib Books.

BIBLIOGRAPHY

Ashrafi, R. (2003). Ethics in Project Management. *IEEE Canadian Review*, Fall 2003: 6–7.

Bredillet, C. (2014). Ethics in Project Management: Some Aristotelian Insights. *International Journal of Managing Projects in Business*, 7(4): 548–565.

Flyvbjerg, B. and Bester, D.W. (2021). The Cost-Benefit Fallacy: Why Cost-Benefit Analysis Is Broken and How to Fix It. *Journal of Benefit-Cost Analysis*, October 2021: 1–25.

Flyvbjerg, B. (2021). Top-Ten Behavioral Biases in Project Management: An Overview. *Project Management Journal*, 52(6): 531–546.

Nalewaik, A. (2020). *Project Cost Recording and Reporting*. Abingdon: Routledge.

Nalewaik, A. and Mills, A. (2016). *Project Performance Review: Capturing the Value of Audit, Oversight, and Compliance for Project Success*. Abingdon: Routledge.

Paul, R. (1990). *Critical Thinking: What Every Person Needs to Survive in a Rapidly Changing World*. Rohnert Park, CA: Center for Critical Thinking and Moral Critique.

Smith, A. (1776), reprint by The Library of Economics and Liberty (2018). *An Inquiry into the Nature and Causes of the Wealth of Nations*. Carmel, IN: Econlib Books.

Sunstein, C. (2000). Cognition and Cost-Benefit Analysis. *The Journal of Legal Studies*, 29(S2): 1059–1103.

The Decision Lab (2024). *Resources: The Decision Lab*. Retrieved on March 12, 2024 from www.thedecisionlab.com.

United States Environmental Protection Agency (2000). *Guidelines for Preparing Economic Analysis*. Washington, DC: Office of the Administrator.

United States Office of Management and Budget (January 11, 1996). *Economic Analysis of Federal Regulations Under Executive Order 12866*. Washington, DC: Executive Office of the President.

Xie, F. and Zhou, T. (2022). Industry Sponsorship Bias in Cost-Effectiveness Analysis: Registry-Based Analysis. The BMJ, 377: e069573.

8

REVIEWING AN ANALYSIS REPORT

The recipient or reader of a strategic project analysis report has an obligation not just to review the report and its conclusions but also to apply critical questioning, identifying shortcomings of the report and seriously considering them in the context of the reader's own intended use of the report data and conclusions. One structured approach is to adopt the stance of a technical peer reviewer when reading the report.

CONTEXT

The first step in reading a report requires understanding its context and, thus, its intent, perspective, and potential biases that shape the report and its conclusions.

Where possible, the reader should identify and comprehend:

1. The funding source for the analysis
2. The perspective from which the analysis was conducted
3. The analysis objective
4. The expected audience for the report
5. The expected use of the report
6. The timing of the report (ex-ante, ex-post, or in medias res) relative to the project schedule

QUALITY

When reading through the report, it is important to also review for report quality and errors. The issues listed below may impede the

DOI: 10.4324/9781003014928-9

reader's understanding of the data and conclusions, and may even intentionally or unintentionally mislead the reader.

The reader should be able to confirm that:

1. Mathematical calculations are attached to the report as an appendix, and are correct.
2. All tables and figures are easy to understand.
3. The report provides an adequate amount of detail, neither obscuring information nor providing too much information.
4. The report appropriately addresses its intended audience and use.
5. The language used in the report is easy to comprehend, and any acronyms are explained
6. The executive summary matches the detailed conclusions in the report.

CRITICAL QUESTIONING

Whereas critical thinking focuses on objective and exploratory reasoning in analysis, critical (or Socratic) questioning is a subset of critical thinking and a disciplined method of reflecting on information received. Critical questioning skills include recognizing ambiguity, probing data to make informed decisions, testing conclusions, challenging assumptions and statements, and identifying flaws, omissions, and inconsistencies. Critical questioning is a necessary step in reading any publication.

The following questions may help the reader better understand both the report and its shortcomings:

1. How many scenarios are included in the analysis?
2. Is the analysis self-contained, or does it supplement other analyses of the same scenarios?
3. Are stakeholders clearly identified, and the determination of standing clearly explained and justified?
4. Does the analysis answer stakeholder questions and address stakeholder issues?
5. Is the selection of the discount rate clearly explained and justified?
6. What is the timeframe in which costs and benefits are analyzed? How is it justified? What is the discount rate effect on benefits, given the timeframe?

7. Is there any weighting applied to scoring? How is it justified?
8. Does the report identify its data sources?
9. Does the report clearly explain the methodologies used for quantification?
10. Was a sensitivity analysis conducted? How does the report reconcile or acknowledge the sensitivity of those variables?
11. How was scenario ranking conducted? Is the methodology clearly explained and justified?
12. Was any part of the analysis conducted by consultants? What are their qualifications?
13. Were any surveys conducted as part of the analysis? Were the surveys attached to the report as an appendix? Review the surveys, if provided, for bias, ambiguity, and leading questions.
14. How clear is the logic, justification, soundness, and relevance of the analysis and conclusions?
15. Does the report identify any unquantified benefits? How are they treated?
16. Are assumptions and omissions identified? Are they clearly explained and justified?
17. Are implications and consequences identified? Are they clearly explained and justified?
18. Is any bias evident?
19. Is any clarification needed?
20. Is there any lack of evidence?

By applying critical questioning while reading a report, the reader can identify and avoid shortcomings of the report and make informed decisions.

REFLECTIONS AND EXERCISES

1. Find two (2) published examples of quantitative or qualitative strategic project analysis. Identify the funding source, perspective, objective, intended audience, and intended use for each. Cite your sources.
2. Find two (2) published examples of quantitative cost-benefit analysis. Try to duplicate the mathematical calculations. Does the report contain sufficient information for you to do so? Why or why not? Cite your sources.

3. Find two (2) published examples of quantitative or qualitative strategic project analysis. Are the tables and figures easy to understand, does the report provide an adequate amount of detail, and does the executive summary correctly represent the detailed conclusions of the report? Why or why not? Cite your sources.
4. Find three (3) published examples, one each of a qualitative, a quantitative, and a blended-approach strategic project analysis. Review the reports critically, and write a two-page reviewer's summary per report. Identify the context, discuss any issues identified, and suggest improvements. Cite your sources.
5. Write five (5) questions to supplement the critical questioning section above.

BIBLIOGRAPHY

Nalewaik, A. (2020). *Project Cost Recording and Reporting*. Abingdon: Routledge.

Nalewaik, A. and Mills, A. (2016). *Project Performance Review: Capturing the Value of Audit, Oversight, and Compliance for Project Success*. Abingdon: Routledge.

Paul, R. (1990). *Critical Thinking: What Every Person Needs to Survive in a Rapidly Changing World*. Rohnert Park, CA: Center for Critical Thinking and Moral Critique.

Xie, F. and Zhou, T. (2022). Industry Sponsorship Bias in Cost-Effectiveness Analysis: Registry-Based Analysis. *The BMJ*, 377: e069573.

9

SUSTAINABILITY AND RESILIENCE

SUSTAINABILITY

The core concept of sustainability is an idealized balance between economic, environmental and societal conditions. The definition of sustainable development is a moving target because it constantly evolves and expands as global society explores the meaning of simultaneously satisfying present and future needs, including what comprises a fundamental 'need' or 'right'.

For example, in 1987 the 'Brundtland' report[1] defined sustainable development as "development that meets the needs of the present without compromising the needs of future generations to meet their own needs". In 2007 the American Society of Civil Engineers (ASCE) defined sustainable development as " . . .the challenge of meeting human needs for natural resources, industrial products, energy, food, transportation, shelter, and waste management while conserving and protecting environmental quality and the natural resource base essential for future development"[2]. In contrast, the ASCE 2023 Policy Statement update defines sustainable development as "a set of economic, environmental and social conditions in which all of society has the capacity and opportunity to maintain and improve its quality of life indefinitely without degrading the quantity, quality or the availability of economic, environmental and social resources"[3].

Over the course of some forty (40) years, the concept of sustainable development has matured and radiated ever outward, like ripples from a stone dropped in water, to include societal and humanitarian needs such as safety, comfort, resilience, well-being, and health, encompassing planet earth and all its living creatures. It

DOI: 10.4324/9781003014928-10

would be neither unreasonable nor unexpected for the definition of sustainable development to eventually reach beyond impacts to planet earth, to consider all space and time and all creatures therein.

The United Nations 2030 Agenda for Sustainable Development is perhaps the most widely recognized guide to sustainability, comprised of seventeen (17) Sustainable Development Goals (SDG), as follows[4]:

1. End poverty in all its forms everywhere.
2. End hunger, achieve food security and improved nutrition, and promote sustainable agriculture.
3. Ensure healthy lives and promote well-being for all at all ages.
4. Ensure inclusive and equitable quality education and promote lifelong learning opportunities for all.
5. Achieve gender equality and empower all women and girls.
6. Ensure availability and sustainable management of water and sanitation for all.
7. Ensure access to affordable, reliable, sustainable and modern energy for all.
8. Promote sustained, inclusive and sustainable economic growth, full and productive employment and decent work for all.
9. Build resilient infrastructure, promote inclusive and sustainable industrialization, and foster innovation.
10. Reduce income inequality within and among countries.
11. Make cities and human settlements inclusive, safe, resilient, and sustainable.
12. Ensure sustainable consumption and production patterns.
13. Take urgent action to combat climate change and its impacts by regulating emissions and promoting developments in renewable energy.
14. Conserve and sustainably use the oceans, seas and marine resources for sustainable development.
15. Protect, restore and promote sustainable use of terrestrial ecosystems, sustainably manage forests, combat desertification, and halt and reverse land degradation and halt biodiversity loss.
16. Promote peaceful and inclusive societies for sustainable development, provide access to justice for all and build effective, accountable and inclusive institutions at all levels.
17. Strengthen the means of implementation and revitalize the Global Partnership for Sustainable Development.

Unfortunately, the limited popular understanding of "sustainability" is that it is primarily related to environmental impacts. The UN SDG goals are so much more than that and can be used as a convenient checklist for identifying societal value benefits for any investment.

RESILIENCE

Resilience is sometimes mentioned in discussions about sustainability and is specifically itemized in UN SDG #9. Like the UN SDGs, the popular understanding of "resilience" is often in the limited context of climate change and flooding. However, resilience is more broadly defined by The Rockefeller Foundation as "the capacity of individuals, communities, institutions, businesses, and systems within a city to survive, adapt, and grow, no matter what kinds of chronic stresses and acute shocks they experience"[5] The philosophy of resilience comes from the concept of ecology, the relationship between living organisms and their physical surroundings. In practice, resilience focuses on adaptability and elasticity in the face of vulnerabilities and any sudden or ongoing change. According to the Rockefeller Foundation, there are four dimensions that contribute to a city's resilience: health and wellbeing, economy and society, infrastructure and environment, and leadership and strategy.

The Rockefeller Foundation has identified twelve (12)[6] goals and fifty-two (52)[7] indicators for the resilience of urban systems, itemized below:

1. Minimal human vulnerability
    a. Safe and accessible housing
    b. Adequate energy supply
    c. Inclusive access to safe drinking water
    d. Effective sanitation
    e. Sufficient food supply
2. Diverse livelihoods and employment
    a. Inclusive labor policies
    b. Relevant skills and training
    c. Dynamic local business development and innovation
    d. Supportive financing mechanisms
    e. Diverse protection of livelihoods following a shock

3. Effective safeguards to human health and life
    a. Robust public health systems
    b. Adequate access to quality healthcare
    c. Well-resourced emergency medical facilities
    d. Effective emergency response services
4. Collective identity and community support
    a. Local community support
    b. Cohesive communities
    c. Strong identify and culture
    d. Actively engaged citizens
5. Comprehensive security and rule of law
    a. Effective systems to deter crime
    b. Proactive corruption prevention
    c. Competent policing
    d. Accessible criminal and civil justice
6. Sustainable economy
    a. Well-managed public finances
    b. Comprehensive business continuity planning
    c. Diverse economic base
    d. Attractive business environment
    e. Strong integration with regional and global economies
7. Reduced exposure and fragility
    a. Comprehensive hazard and exposure mapping
    b. Appropriate codes, standards, and enforcement
    c. Effectively managed protective ecosystems
    d. Robust protective infrastructure
8. Effective provision of critical services
    a. Effective stewardship of ecosystems
    b. Flexible infrastructure
    c. Retained redundant capacity
    d. Balanced supply and demand of resources
    e. Diligent maintenance and continuity
    f. Adequate continuity for critical assets and services
9. Reliable mobility and communications
    a. Diverse and affordable transport networks
    b. Effective transport operation and maintenance
    c. Reliable communication technology
    d. Secure technology networks

10. Effective leadership and management
    a. Appropriate government decision-making
    b. Effective coordination with other government bodies
    c. Proactive multi-stakeholder collaboration
    d. Comprehensive hazard monitoring and risk assessment
    e. Comprehensive emergency management
11. Empowered stakeholders
    a. Adequate education for all
    b. Widespread community awareness and preparedness
    c. Effective mechanisms for communities to engage with the city government
12. Integrated development and planning
    a. Comprehensive city monitoring and data management
    b. Consultative planning process
    c. Appropriate land use and zoning
    d. Robust planning approval process

There is significant overlap between the goals of sustainability and resilience, although by being less specific in wording the Rockefeller Foundation resilience goals succeed in being conceptually broader than the United Nations goals. Like the UN SDGs, the Rockefeller Foundation's list of resilience goals can be used as a convenient checklist for identifying societal value benefits for any investment.

If the definition of "resources" includes more than just financial expenditures, expanding to include health, systems, people, time, energy, materials, and more, the optimization of resource use is also implicit in the concepts and goals of sustainability and resilience. The combination of sustainability and resilience concepts creates a framework for the assessment of public and private initiatives and government policymaking, and the identification of societal value benefits.

The need for funding for studies that can quantify, price, and/or shadow price sustainability and resilience benefits is well known, and the knowledge gap persists. Part of the challenge is one of budgeting, presuming a fixed amount of available (presumably annual) funding for public, private, and nonprofit sector entities alike. The other challenge is one of temporal scope. Many sustainability and resilience benefits take years, if not generations, to be realized. The likelihood of any entity to fund a reliable multi-generational (longitudinal) study is incredibly slim, given the decades of resources required and the cost. Studies conducted are more likely to be retrospective and ex-post than prospective. Retrospective studies consider what has happened, and attempt to collect appropriate available data, often through interviews and review of records. Prospective studies occur at the same time as the change in desired characteristics. For a prospective longitudinal study to be conducted, funding must be allocated for a multi-year effort, and desired sustainability and resilience outcomes must be specifically identified at the outset of the study, then measured at prescribed time intervals using specific and consistent data-gathering methods.

REFLECTIONS AND EXERCISES

1. Explain in your own words how sustainability and resilience overlap. Provide two (2) examples not already mentioned.
2. Explain in your own words where sustainability and resilience diverge. Provide two (2) examples not already mentioned.
3. What types of sustainability benefits and disbenefits might be difficult to quantify? Explain.
4. What types of resilience benefits and disbenefits might be difficult to quantify? Explain.
5. Can you identify any additional societal value benefits that are not listed in the sustainability and resilience goals? Explain.

NOTES

1 World Commission on Environment and Development. (1987). *Report of the WCED: Our Common Future*. Oslo: General Assembly of the United Nations.

2 American Society of Civil Engineers. (2007). *The Role of the Civil Engineer in Sustainable Development*. Reston VA: American Society of Civil Engineers.

3 American Society of Civil Engineers. (2023). *Policy Statement 418: The Role of the Civil Engineer in Sustainable Development*. Reston, VA: American Society of Civil Engineers.

4 United Nations (2015). *Transforming Our World: The 2030 Agenda for Sustainable Development*. A/RES/70/1. New York: Division for Social Development Goals, United Nations Department of Economic and Social Affairs.

5 The Rockefeller Foundation. (2013). *City Resilience Index*. Retrieved on February 24, 2024 from www.rockefellerfoundation.org/report/city-resilience-index-2.

6 City Resilience Index (2018). *City Resilience Index*. Retrieved on February 24, 2024 from www.cityresilienceindex.org/#.

7 Arup International Development. (2016). *CRI Research Report Volume 6/6: Measurement Guide*. New York: The Rockefeller Foundation.

BIBLIOGRAPHY

American Society of Civil Engineers. (2007). *The Role of the Civil Engineer in Sustainable Development*. Reston VA: American Society of Civil Engineers.

American Society of Civil Engineers. (2023). *Policy Statement 418: The Role of the Civil Engineer in Sustainable Development*. Reston, VA: American Society of Civil Engineers.

Arup International Development. (2016). *CRI Research Report Volume 6/6: Measurement Guide*. New York: The Rockefeller Foundation.

City Resilience Index (2018). *City Resilience Index*. Retrieved on February 24, 2024 from www.cityresilienceindex.org/#.

Sinden, A. (2019). *The Problem of Unquantified Benefits*. Environmental Law, 49(1), 73–129.

The Rockefeller Foundation. (2013). *City Resilience Index*. Retrieved on February 24, 2024 from www.rockefellerfoundation.org/report/city-resilience-index-2.

United Nations (2015). *Transforming Our World: The 2030 Agenda for Sustainable Development*. A/RES/70/1. New York: Division for Social Development Goals, United Nations Department of Economic and Social Affairs.

Wise, R.M. et al. (2022). *Pragmatic Cost-Benefit Analysis for Infrastructure Resilience. Nature Climate Change*, 12, 881–883.

World Commission on Environment and Development. (1987). *Report of the WCED: Our Common Future*. Oslo: General Assembly of the United Nations.

10

SCENARIOS

CONSTRUCTION

The type of benefits and disbenefits identified for construction projects varies significantly by the type of facility and the category of ownership (public, private, NGO), as discussed next.

Targeted services

Public benefit programs and international development initiatives are created with the intent for capacity-building and the realization of outcomes (merit goods) that influence human health and well-being by providing the infrastructure for critical services and utilities, reducing poverty and hunger, improving education, improving health and well-being, and combating climate change. Merit goods are products and services that are deemed socially desirable, often provided to specific societal groups by the public or private sector for free or at a discounted (subsidized) rate; examples include food, education, healthcare, public transportation, and social housing. These scenarios create societal value owing to the intrinsic nature of their existence. As such, target sustainability and resilience benefits are typically identified in the analysis, although additional unexpected benefits (known as fortuitous benefits) may also occur.

Because methodologies have been developed and some studies conducted for both the ex-ante quantification and ex-post measurement of certain such benefits, those benefits tend to be costed or otherwise shadow-priced or metricized in societal scenario analysis. The entity conducting the analysis may have a well-established process and quality control mechanism for the work and may conduct

DOI: 10.4324/9781003014928-11

similar analyses frequently such that they are able to reference past reports and be reasonably efficient in the process.

It is increasingly common in evaluation to conduct quantitative analysis either after a project has already been selected using other (qualitative) methods or after the project has been completed (ex-post). Ex-ante analysis of World Bank projects was performed for 70 percent of projects in 1970, compared to only 25 percent in 2008[1]. This is due largely to legitimate difficulties in obtaining data and applying rigorous cost-benefit analysis (CBA) and similar quantitative methods.

Public infrastructure

Much of the discussion of the benefits for public infrastructure projects classified as public goods focuses on jobs created, human capital development, and environmental impact. Public goods are products and services that are accessible to all, such that usage or consumption by one user does not preclude usage or consumption by someone else. Public goods are often funded through taxation or user fees; examples include infrastructure such as rail transport and national defense.

Major infrastructure projects typically use consultant services to perform the analysis, and the consultant firm and available staff might not be the same year after year owing to competitive sourcing. The senior staff named in the proposal for the work might be substituted by junior staff, in a bait-and-switch common to consulting firm behavior in an effort to reduce the internal cost of the work. Productivity, relevant experience and capability, integrity, and diligence are invisible to the infrastructure owner and/or their agent, typical of the principal-agent problem inherent in consultant-owner relationships. As such, the quality, contents, and output from the analysis will vary year over year.

The use of shadow pricing in major infrastructure analysis is somewhat rare, as is the use of Likert or similar scoring. What can be easily quantified will be costed, but the consultant is also on a fixed budget and not inclined to overrun their allotted hours for the effort; the breadth and depth of analysis will always be bounded to match the consulting contract price. It is unlikely the consultant firm will conduct studies to craft appropriate shadow pricing, unless that work is explicitly part of the contract scope and priced accordingly.

For example, California High-Speed Rail project CBAs (updated in 2008[2], 2014[3], and 2023[4]) focused on a 50-year time period for benefits and disbenefits such as residual value, stations and train amenities, land-take disbenefits (agricultural productivity loss and wetland loss), and State and National environmental objectives such as renewable power, airline trip reduction (reduced fuel and operations costs, reduced passenger and airline delays, reduced emissions), tree programs, and road vehicle trip reduction (improved safety and reliability, productivity increases, net reduced noise and air pollution, reduced travel time and vehicle operating cost, reduced oil imports, and reduced parking infrastructure). The analyses specifically excluded disbenefits during construction, land use and property value impacts, effects on urban rail corridors and other transit systems, and disbenefits to cities without a planned train station (community severance). Also excluded were benefits and disbenefits to be identified in a separate environmental impact report (EIR). Job creation, wage uplift, economic growth, and other macroeconomic concepts could be found in the separate Economic Impact Analysis (EIA) Report. Similarly, actual-to-date economic investment, breakeven analysis, small businesses engaged, construction jobs created, benefits to disadvantaged communities, greenhouse gas emissions removed, lifetime construction emission offsets, and habitat lands restored or preserved were included as part of the annual business plan update, along with the aforementioned EIR, EIA, and CBA.[5].

Similarly, a Sound Transit BCA report for a rail project specifically excluded reliability, impacts on employment, operations costs, and maintenance costs, impacts to property values, transit fares, generative transit effects, parking cost savings, unpriced parking, and Federal funds to be received.[6]

Essentially, the CBA analyses for such major public capital investments typically perform quantification of costs, benefits, and disbenefits that are easy to monetize and defend, and less likely to be subjective and thus controversial. It is worth noting that each decade's iteration of the CAHSR CBA expanded the number and type of costs and benefits identified, perhaps evolving in line with the rest of the infrastructure construction industry and/or reflecting the capabilities of and data available to the consultant firm performing the analysis.

Public infrastructure has been increasing its endorsement of sustainable development and social procurement during both construction and operations. Social procurement seeks to address sustainability goals while performing ethical sourcing throughout the supply chain. In public construction, it is not unusual for an owner entity to conduct outreach to and enable contracting/subcontracting opportunities for small, disadvantaged, minority, woman-owned, and veteran-owned businesses, provide estimating and bidding training to those businesses, and create internships and apprenticeships to build local construction labor (human capital) capacity.

Projects may also consider benefits from circular economy initiatives as part of sustainable development planning. The circular economy (referred to in popular culture by the phrase "reduce, reuse, recycle") focuses on minimizing waste and using materials and products in a sustainable manner. In construction, this may mean selecting comparable products that meet the project requirements but are made from recycled materials, reusing materials generated during the demolition phase, selecting materials that have a cradle-to-cradle lifecycle, embracing modular practices, and designing for increased durability.

Ex-post analysis may be required by law; Post-Opening Project Evaluation (POPE) is performed for United Kingdom transport projects, "Before and After Studies of New Starts" in the United States, and similar in Norway and France. Such studies tend to focus on construction costs, traffic forecasts (travel time and vehicle operating cost savings), and safety. The analysis will also consider the planned and actual cost and schedule for the project, and profitability. Unplanned benefits might or might not be included in the analysis and report. One challenge in ex-post analysis of transport infrastructure, specifically, is establishing a counter-factual scenario in which the project was never built (the do-nothing option), against which to compare the current situation. This involves a pseudo-historical reconstruction of the past, retroactively "forecasting" a realistic yet possible regional economy, traffic and shipping growth, employment, business growth, land use, and more, except the scenario is that of a non-actual world without the existence of the transport project. A second obstacle in performing an ex-post transport analysis occurs because there may be a mismatch between the time frame used for the ex-ante analysis (typically 20–25 years) and the point in time at which the ex-post analysis is required (typically after one or five years of operation). This may mean that the ex-post analysis must both capture past data and perform a forecast to the endpoint of the ex-ante analysis, effectively turning the ex-post analysis into an in-medias res analysis.

Private investment

In contrast, private construction projects, such as buildings for manufacturing and commercial uses, often fall short and lack sophistication in the identification of benefits, let alone the quantification of those benefits; analysis is almost exclusively financial/economic, focused on return on investment. If benefits are identified, they typically focus heavily on green building certification for buildings and environmental impact. Note that, for construction projects, an environmental impact analysis is typically a prerequisite for permitting and project approval; thus, the analysis benefits from a separate (mandatory) study. If the owner is pursuing local government subsidies for land acquisition, construction, or operations, the analysis may also include the number of temporary and permanent jobs created and a quantification of other economic impacts.

To the casual observer, sustainable development in construction is about solar panels, water-efficient landscaping, natural lighting and ventilation, bike paths, and (last but definitely not least) the positive public image, marketability, value increase, and goodwill created by obtaining green building certification. A more informed audience is likely aware that green building certification rewards total life-cycle cost savings, improvements in occupant health and comfort, and positive effects on worker productivity and quality of life. The United States Green Building Council (USGBC) and other certifying bodies have been necessarily responsive to the changing global understanding of sustainability, such as the Paris Agreement adopted at the UN Climate Change Conference (COP21) in 2015. As such, the USGBC has continually evolved the Leadership in Energy and Environmental Design (LEED) Green Building Rating SystemTM and certification[7], which now includes health and human impacts such as physical, mental, and behavioral well-being, societal equity, economic and community benefits, and resilience.

However, improvements in the identification of sustainability benefits and social procurement efforts have not always necessarily translated to the inclusion and quantification of those elements in

CBAs. This is likely because green building certification, circular economy elements, and social procurement are planned during the design phase of construction and not achieved until the completion of construction and start of operations, whereas strategic project analysis is typically conducted during the project feasibility stage with only a very basic design outline. In such instances, new data may be used to update the original analysis when more information becomes available, or actual data may be utilized in a more comprehensive ex-post analysis.

SCIENCE AND TECHNOLOGY

Science and technology projects are typically very unique, representing leaps in concept. Infrastructure may be physical (buildings, equipment) or virtual (databases, e-facilities), stand-alone (single purpose and users) or shared (multiple purpose and users). Often, the technology has never before been developed or deployed. There may be a lack of competition in the market, by design; astrophysics and space science projects, specifically, are conceived to complement each other and broaden the globally available research infrastructure, avoiding competition with each other. As such, these projects are very difficult to price, and there is often little historic data available, information may be outdated, and/or there may be no point of reference for project cost and schedule. The facilities are often operational for several generations, as the lifetime of major science equipment is often extended through the addition of new generations of instruments.

Estimates for such projects are well known for being wildly incorrect, with extreme cost and schedule overruns. Part of this is because science, technology, and research projects are unique, with no or few available sources of cost data. They are difficult to cost and plan. But there is a bigger, systemic reason for the overruns. Although government-funded science projects are designed for synergy, they all still pull funds from the same available pot of money, typically in one-year increments. This funding process creates several problems. First, it incentivizes low estimates; no matter how strong the argument is for project selection based on purpose, the funding agency is not blind to the proposed cost and may be inclined to fund a large handful of low-cost projects instead of a select few big ones.

This selection process spreads the available monies more equitably across multiple disciplines and institutions and will result in a higher and more diverse yield of research outcomes. Everybody wins . . . except the big projects. However, this process leads to the second problem (or benefit, depending on one's perspective). Dividing spending into smaller annual increments means dividing the project work into bite-size pieces. This effectively spreads out the total work over a longer period of time; publicly funded science and technology projects could potentially be completed more quickly and at lower cost, were they to receive more funding earlier in the project lifecycle. Research institutions benefit from piecemeal funding and a long timeline because the process levels out (flattens) what would otherwise have been a "normal curve" of effort and, thus, expenditure and employment. Instead of suffering peaks and valleys of existence, such research institutions plod along somewhat comfortably. This leads us to the disbenefit side of the situation: the annual funding mechanism increases the total outturn cost of the project because each piece of deferred funding is subject to additional (possibly unnecessary) inflation and risk.

In previous decades, national security and military applications from research output and industry spillover effects were the primary justification for major public investment in science and technology, and the military-industrial-academic complex played a large role in such projects. In financial analysis, a spillover effect refers to unintended positive or negative network effects and consequences from an activity (or changes in activity), policymaking, or occurrences such as consumer spending, pollution, or a pandemic. The effects may be economic, societal, or political. In scientific and research investment scenarios, knowledge spillovers are externalities that occur in firms, industries, technological clusters, or geographic areas outside the scientific institution that originated the knowledge, owing to an exchange of ideas. Knowledge spillovers result in the rapid propagation of learning and innovations, yield process improvements and efficiencies, and increase entrepreneurship and economic growth through product and process developments and industrial-technological transfer that eventually reach the military, government, private sector, and public sector (in that specific order) for use. There are numerous other outputs and benefits from radio astronomy research that are non-quantifiable but are still considered valuable, such as: science diplomacy, public policy advisory, and improved trust in science.

The post-Cold War (current) trend in primary justification for major public investment in science and technology (specifically big science or mega-science) is knowledge creation and big data generation as public goods. Owing to the very nature of research, benefits are anticipated as part of the knowledge-creation and innovation processes, but there is no guarantee that benefits will occur, nor is any market yet identified for future discoveries and associated benefits. Scientific discovery is unique in that it has non-use value but holds the promise of future-use benefits in service to society. Further, the financial benefits received from such projects will almost never exceed the initial investment cost of billions or even trillions of dollars to develop the infrastructure, even with donated or heavily subsidized land, building, and equipment costs. Construction costs (the initial investment) typically eclipse operations costs (the ongoing investment).

For the same budgetary and time requirements as mentioned in Chapter 9 of this book for sustainability and resilience benefits, there have been few longitudinal prospective studies of science and technology projects. Benefits created by research projects also require decades, if not generations, to be realized and it is often difficult to trace a direct path or identify causation between discovery and innovation because outcomes are nonlinear. Retrospective studies have identified many societal value benefits, but typically have not quantified those or developed shadow pricing.

As a result, the quantification of benefits for CBAs is often restricted to broader impacts (BI) such as education opportunities and the resultant improvements in science, technology, engineering, and math (STEM) skills, citizen science, raised awareness of science, public outreach, and STEM human capacity development (such as increases in the number of K-12 school graduates, university graduates, graduate students, number of PhDs awarded, recent graduates in new scientific careers, etc.). The number of temporary and permanent jobs at the facility will be quantified and costed, along with the quantification of other measurable outputs such as the number of publications, citations, projects conducted, grants received, and scientific users of the infrastructure.

Economic development studies will typically be performed, which may include analysis of jobs created, and benefits and revenue from licenses and patents, consultancy and advisory services, rental of physical space, education and outreach fees, procurement and research contracts, local expenditures and business growth, domestic and foreign direct investment, grants, industry partnerships, and international trade. Science tourism might be included in the economic analysis. Environmental impact reports (required for construction) will typically be provided for physical science and technology infrastructure, which include analysis of benefits and disbenefits to land, water, air, and living beings (creatures, plants, etc.).

Radio astronomy observatories

Much of what is known about science and technology project benefits is due not to CBA and other ex-ante studies but to ex-post societal, environmental, and economic impact analysis. Ultimately, the socio-economic impact is considerably broader than mere scientific output, and is both nationally transformative and generational, yet these benefits are not often quantified during the project justification phase. This may be due to the politics of science project approval, discussed below.

Foreign and private investment are often included in the project proposal, as multi-national, multi-disciplinary, and inter-organization cooperation are typical for major telescope projects; big science projects are prohibitively expensive, with much of the funding invested in advanced technology and development of the physical infrastructure. The nature of the scientific astrophysics community is such that a pipeline of global telescope projects is continually maintained to ensure employment and the continuation of both the research economy and established institutions. This has led to multiple carefully crafted narratives that vary depending on the context and audience. Whereas the internal justification for a project may be purely strategic, the external justification for project approval may require tactical framing as a niche facility (the Gemini telescopes in Hawaii and Chile), military apparatus (Jodrell Bank laid claim to ballistic missile tracking capabilities), or even presentation as something else entirely to access a different source of funds (Low-Frequency Array, LOFAR, was proposed as an information technology project).

The location requirements for radio astronomy observatories simplify the identification of societal, environmental, and economic impacts resulting from the construction of a major scientific installation. The nature of the research and equipment requires cold and dry atmospheric conditions, low light pollution, and low electromagnetic interference. As such, the location of such infrastructure is often very remote, making incremental changes and direct cause-and-effect in environmental impact, community well-being, and economic growth much easier to measure than similar effects for other types of infrastructure projects.

The author recently conducted an ex-post study of radio astronomy observatories in seven (7) countries, identifying additional benefits that can be categorized according to their origins in related infrastructure and research, in addition to the numerous economic and research output benefits identified above[8]. These are discussed below.

Physical infrastructure

The physical installations required for modern radio astronomy sites include the buildings, utilities, and other infrastructure to support not just the antennas but also the installed equipment, staff working at the site, operations and maintenance personnel, and visitors. Such buildings may include laboratories, chilled equipment areas, caged equipment areas to protect from electromagnetic interference, offices, meeting rooms, break rooms, reception desk, library, auditorium, visitor area and store, exhibits, maintenance shops, storage areas, temporary accommodations for staff, and more.

Benefits related to the construction of physical research infrastructure included temporary jobs, development of construction trade skills, growth of local businesses to supply construction materials and labor, and new and improved roads and other civil infrastructure such as water supply, electric utilities, sewerage, and waste facilities. On occasion, a nature reserve was created to allow a natural buffer surrounding the facilities, creating natural habitats and other ecological benefits. Disbenefits included restrictions on telecommunication and aviation, land acquisition, and related agricultural economy impacts and job losses.

Other physical and services infrastructure in the community resulted from the existence of the research facility and personnel, such as short- and long-term housing, new and improved local schools, universities, libraries, healthcare facilities and services, transportation services, other public goods such as fire, emergency, and police services, community centers, and more. Such infrastructure, over a generational timeframe, was interpreted to yield improved community health and well-being. Population growth may also have occurred as a result of entrepreneurship, business creation, and job opportunities.

Operations infrastructure

The infrastructure for research usually includes necessary facilities and services for ongoing operations, administration, management, and maintenance. Benefits related to the operations of physical and virtual research infrastructure included maintenance and housekeeping vocational skills development, professional skills development in mechanical engineering, systems engineering, data science, machine learning, and software development, permanent and contract jobs, and local business growth to supply parts, materials, equipment, services, labor, hospitality, and food. Population growth may also have occured as a result of entrepreneurship, business creation, and job opportunities.

Infrastructure applications

The antennas and equipment installed as part of the radio astronomy array are useful to many areas of science and research beyond that of astronomy, and the physical facilities, antennas, and equipment can be made available to visiting scientists from other disciplines. Research has been conducted in food, forestry, fisheries, and agriculture, environmental protection and biodiversity, climate change, air and water resources, land monitoring and management, healthcare, cultural heritage, paleontology and archaeology, and military applications. Benefits related to the use of research and equipment infrastructure by other disciplines included improvements in local, national, and international community and environmental health and wellbeing, along with research outputs such as broader impacts, scientific discoveries, spillover effects, and industrial-technological transfer.

CULTURAL OUTPUT

The research output from radio astronomy occasionally inspires the development of cultural goods and benefits such as books, music, movies, fine arts and photography. The facility itself and related research tend to attract tourism (astrotourism), inspiring entrepreneurship and local business growth to support hospitality and restaurants. Additional shops, services, festivals, museums, and attractions may also develop, related to local (often indigenous) culture, historic and culturally significant sites, native flora and fauna, and other leisure activities available in the area. All these, ultimately, were identified as benefits to both the local community and region.

Space-based solar power

The next example is less about what has been achieved in science and technology projects than what might be achieved in the future. This is an illustration of climate change (net zero) goals inspiring creative technical solutions.

Several recent preliminary studies of space-based solar power were conducted in the United Kingdom,[9] Europe,[10] and the United States[11]. The studies considered (to various degrees) the costs, risks, constraints, opportunities, and financial and technological feasibility of space-based solar power. The studies also included calculations of energy demand through to 2050 with decommissioning from 2070 until 2075, compared the proposed scenarios to the cost and environmental impact of existing electricity production technologies, and identified additional benefits that can be categorized by impact type. These benefits are discussed below.

First, some background. In theory, the process for harvesting space-based solar power is shown below.

It was generally accepted that the process is cost-prohibitive and a financing gap exists such that public funds will need to be supplemented

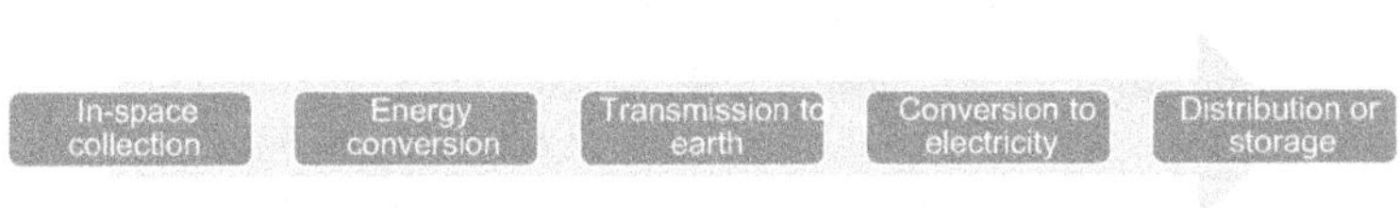

Figure 10.1 Space-based solar power

by private investment, with the caveat that future innovation, technology, and engineering may reduce some of that risk. Some elements of the process may even be technically infeasible at this time, with potentially significant but as-yet-unknown disbenefits. Again, future innovation, technology, and engineering may reduce some of those issues and risks.

Calculations used in the CBA included NPV, B/C, and the levelized cost of electricity (LCOE), defined as the revenue required to recover lifecycle costs and break even, divided by the amount of electricity produced over the same period. A simulation model was used to create a variation on LCOE; value-adjusted LCOE (VALCOE) was utilized to compare different power generation technologies not just on cost but also in terms of energy, capacity, and flexibility. Key metrics included mass (the primary driver for the cost of space launches), efficiency, and cost. A system value framework was used to assess other quantitative and qualitative benefits, including socio-political-economic benefits, STEM impact, net zero goals, and more.

Strategic benefits

Although climate change (net zero) goals were a primary driver for the space-based solar power concept, strategic national benefits such as increased energy independence (reduced imports) and technology leadership were highly prized. The value of global partnerships and international collaboration was also mentioned.

Economic benefits

The process was expected to generate cost reductions which were quantified and monetized in the analysis, such as reductions in the use of land-based electricity generation, reduced cost of imported fuel, and potentially lower energy costs (which presumably ignored the significant initial investment). Any excess energy generated was seen to have export potential.

A large number of economic benefits identified were related to the development of a space economy, technology spillover (which was monetized in the analysis) and advancements in the technology, commercial, and manufacturing industries. Impacts to robotics, photovoltaics, wireless power transmission, semiconductors, and autonomous systems were specifically identified. Benefits related to the construction of physical infrastructure included temporary and permanent jobs, and the development of high-value skilled labor, which were quantified in the analysis. Business growth was also predicted (and quantified in the analysis) in industries such as space grade electronics, robotic assembly, and commercial space freight and travel.

Economic disbenefits were identified, which included the cost of developing the technology and potential conflicts with the space location of other satellites.

Societal benefits

In addition to employment, health benefits from pollution reduction (including visual and noise pollution) were projected, along with increased safety for operations in space owing to the use of robots. Increases in public acceptance of space technology and innovation for the benefit of humanity (with impacts to STEM fields and academia) were also identified as societal benefits.

One societal disbenefit (and potentially high risk) identified was the unknown impacts to human health owing to energy transmission from space.

Environmental benefits

The analyses quantified but took different approaches with monetizing (or not monetizing) environmental benefits such as lower greenhouse gas emissions and reduced requirements for raw material supplies and fossil fuels.

Numerous environmental disbenefits were identified, including the environmental impacts of construction and space launch, the amount of land required for earth-based facilities (which were quantified as opportunity costs), the space waste created at the time of disposal owing to graveyard orbit, and (similar to the societal disbenefit mentioned above) the unknown environmental impacts owing to energy transmission from space.

As with construction, the CBA analyses for space-based solar power investments performed quantification of costs, benefits, and disbenefits that were easy to monetize and defend, and less likely to be subjective and thus controversial. The lack of longitudinal studies of science and technology projects, generational timeline for certain benefits, and nonlinearity of innovation outcomes were all certainly a factor in the choice of elements to quantify and monetize. As with radio astronomy projects, economic development studies were key to the analyses.

POLICYMAKING

Although policymaking often requires a CBA (by law), evidence shows that policymaking tends to fall woefully short in quantifying sustainability and resilience benefits.

A study of environmental policy CBAs concluded that 80 percent of the US Environmental Protection Agency CBAs over a thirteen (13)-year period excluded benefits considered important, significant, or substantial to the analysis owing to data limitations and an inability to perform meaningful quantification and calculation of those benefits. Excluding these benefits resulted in very low benefit estimates clearly outweighed by quantified costs, yielding an unbalanced or even illegitimate CBA. In certain instances, the analysis managed to omit the "value of ameliorating the very harm at which the rule itself was aimed."[12]

Such studies have determined the problem of unquantified benefits is systemic and pervasive in policymaking, a conclusion that can easily be extended to construction and some public benefit programs and international development initiatives.

REFLECTIONS AND EXERCISES

1. Explain in your own words why costs, benefits, and disbenefits are difficult to identify and quantify for unique projects. Provide two (2) examples not already mentioned.
2. List thirty-five (35) categories of potential costs, benefits, and disbenefits for a new toll road.
3. What types of costs, benefits, and disbenefits might be identified for a privatized space science project in an ex-post analysis, but not in an ex-ante analysis? Explain.
4. Identify some recent legislation or societal initiative that has affected you. Identify, explain, and quantify the impacts to yourself.
5. Identify a recent construction project that is local to you. Identify, explain, and quantify the impacts to yourself.

NOTES

1 IEG (2010). *Cost-Benefit Analysis in World Bank Projects*. Fast Track Brief, 57037, June 4, 2010. Washington, DC: World Bank.
2 Cambridge Systematics (2008). *Benefit-Cost Analysis*. Sacramento, CA: California High-Speed Rail Authority.
3 Parsons Brinckerhoff (2014). *2014 California High-Speed Rail Benefit-Cost Analysis*. Sacramento: California High-Speed Rail Authority.
4 KPMG (2023). *2023 Benefit-Cost Analysis*. Sacramento, CA: California High-Speed Rail Authority.
5 CAHSRA (2024). *2024 Revised Draft Business Plan*. Sacramento: California High-Speed Rail Authority.
6 Sound Transit (2015). *ST3 Regional High-Capacity Transit System Plan: Benefit-Cost Analysis Methodology Report*. Seattle, WA: Sound Transit.
7 USGBC (2025). *Leadership in Energy and Environmental Design (LEED) Green Building Rating SystemTM . version 5*. Atlanta GA: U.S. Green Building Council.
8 Nalewaik, A. and Williams, N. (2021). *Emergent and Unexpected Sources of Value from Radio Astronomy Projects*. New York: 2021 IEEE European Technology and Engineering Management Summit (E-TEMS).
9 Frazer-Nash Consultancy and London Economics (2022). *Space-Based Solar Power: A Future Source of Energy for Europe? A study conducted for the European Space Agency.* Retrieved on February 7, 2024 from www.fnc.co.uk/media/fi4pvbgv/space-based-solar-power-final-report.pdf.
10 Berger, R. (2022). *Space-Based Solar Power: Can it Help to Decarbonize Europe and Make it More Energy Resilient? A study conducted for the European Space Agency*. Retrieved on February 7, 2024 from www.rolandberger.com/en/Insights/Publications/Space-based-Solar-Power.html.
11 Office of Technology, Policy, and Strategy (2024). *Space-Based Solar Power.* Washington, DC: NASA.
12 Sinden, A. (2019). The Problem of Unquantified Benefits. *Environmental Law*, 49(1): 73–129.

BIBLIOGRAPHY

Agar, J. (1998). *Science & Spectacle: The Work of Jodrell Bank in Post-War British Culture*. Amsterdam: Harwood Academic Publishers.

Arup International Development. (2016). *CRI Research Report Volume 6/6: Measurement Guide*. New York: The Rockefeller Foundation.

Atkinson, D. et al. (2017). *Socio-economic Assessment of SKA Phase 1 in South Africa*. Cape Town: South African Radio Astronomy Observatory.

Baneke, D. (2020). Let's Not Talk About Science. *Science, Technology, & Human Values*, 45(1): 164–194.

Baneke, D. (2023). Big Astronomy: Large Telescopes and the Dual Narrative of Impact. In: Charitos, P. et al (Eds.), *Big Science in the 21st Century*. Bristol: IOP Publishing.

Battistoni, G., et al. (2016). Cost-Benefit Analysis of Applied Research Infrastructure: Evidence from Health Care. *Technological Forecasting & Social Change*, 112: 79–91.

Breese, R., Jenner, S., Serra, C., and Thorp, J. (2015). Benefits Management: Lost or Found in Translation. *International Journal of Project Management*, 33(7): 1438–1451.

Bunduchi, R., Weisshaar, C. & Smart, A.U. (2011). Mapping the Benefits and Costs Associated with Process Innovation: The Case of RFID Adoption. *Technovation*, 31(9): 505–521.

Butković, L.L., et al. (2023). *The Benefits of Cost-Benefit Analysis in Construction Projects.* 6th IPMA SENET Project Management Conference. Dubrovnik: International Project Management Association.

CAHSRA (2024). *2024 Revised Draft Business Plan*. Sacramento, CA: California High-Speed Rail Authority.

Cambridge Systematics (2008). *Benefit-Cost Analysis*. Sacramento, CA: California High-Speed Rail Authority.

Chaudhary, S.K. (2023). A Review of Evaluation Methodologies and Techniques in Construction Engineering Projects. *International Journal of Construction Engineering and Management*, 12(2): 35–42.

City Resilience Index (2018). *City Resilience Index*. Retrieved on February 24, 2024 from www.cityresilienceindex.org/#/

Coccia, M. (2018). *Socioeconomic Driving Forces of Scientific Research*. Moncalieri: CocciaLab at CNR.

Comptroller General of the United States (1972). *Report to the Congress: Cost-Benefit Analysis Used in Support of the Space Shuttle Program*. Washington, DC: NASA.

De Brucker, K. et al. (1995). The Economic Evaluation of Public Investments in Transport Infrastructure: The Use of Multicriteria Analysis. *International Journal of Transport Economics*, 22(3): 261–281.

de Rus, G. et al. (2023). Cost–Benefit Analysis of Transport Investments: An Application to High-Speed Rail Investments. In: de Rus, G. et al. (Eds.), *Economic Evaluation of Transport Projects*. Berlin: Springer

Duncan, C. (2014). *Incorporating Qualitative Factors in Transportation Decision-Making.* Retrieved on October 17, 2023 from Economic Development Research Group. www.ebp-us.com/en/blog/incorporating-qualitative-factors-transportation-decision-making.

Elzinga, A. (2012). The Current Science Policy Regime: Viewed in Historical Perspective. *Science and Public Policy*, 39: 416–428.

Florio, M. and Vignetti, S. (2013). *The Use of Ex Post Cost-Benefit Analysis to Assess the Long-Term Effects of Major Infrastructure Projects*. Centre for Industrial Studies, Working Paper N. 02/2013.

Florio, M. (2019). *Investing in Science: Social Cost-Benefit Analysis of Research Infrastructure*. Cambridge, MA: The MIT Press.

Florio, M. (2021). Knowledge Creation: New Frontiers for Public Investment. *Annals of Public and Cooperative Economics*, 92: 379–386.

Frazer-Nash Consultancy and London Economics (2022). *Space-Based Solar Power: A Future Source of Energy for Europe? A study conducted for the European Space Agency.* Retrieved on February 7, 2024 from www.fnc.co.uk/media/fi4pvbgv/space-based-solar-power-final-report.pdf.

Frischmann, B.M. (2012). *Infrastructure: The Social Value of Shared Resources.* New York: Oxford University Press.

Griniece, E. et al. (2020). *The Guidebook for Socio-Economic Impact Assessment of Research Infrastructures.* Brussels: Research Infrastructure Impact Assessment paTHwayS (RI PATHS) Consortium.

Heeschen, D.S. (February 22, 1972). *Letter from D.S. Heeschen (NRAO) to Daniel F. Hunt (NSF).* Charlottesville, VA: National Radio Astronomy Observatory Archives.

IEG (2010). *Cost-Benefit Analysis in World Bank Projects.* Fast Track Brief, 57037, June 4, 2010. Washington, DC: World Bank.

Kockelman, K. (1994). High-Speed Rail in California: A Cost-Benefit Analysis. *Berkeley Planning Journal*, 9: 61–80.

KPMG (2023). *2023 Benefit-Cost Analysis.* Sacramento, CA: California High-Speed Rail Authority.

Laird, J., Nash, C., and Mackie, P. (2014). Transformational Transport Infrastructure: Cost-Benefit Analysis Challenges. *The Town Planning Review*, 85(6), 709–730.

Lewis Research Center (1976). *NASA Technical Memorandum X-3453: Cost-Benefit Analysis of Space Technology*. Washington, DC: NASA.

Lock, D. (Ed.) (2021). *The Practitioner Handbook of Project Controls.* Abingdon: Routledge.

McCray, W.P. (2000). Large Telescopes and the Moral Economy of Recent Astronomy. *Social Studies of Science*, (30)5: 685–711.

Nalewaik, A. and Williams, N. (2021). *Emergent and Unexpected Sources of Value from Radio Astronomy Projects*. New York: 2021 IEEE European Technology and Engineering Management Summit (E-TEMS).

Nicolaisen, M.S. and Driscoll, P.A. (2016). An International Review of Ex-Post Evaluation Schemes in the Transport Sector. *Journal of Environmental Assessment Policy and Management*, (10)1: 1–33.

OECD Secretariat (2019). *OECD Science, Technology, and Industry Policy Paper No. 65: Reference Framework for Assessing the Scientific and Socio-Economic Impact of Research Infrastructures*. Paris: OECD Publishing.

Office of Technology, Policy, and Strategy (2023). *Cost and Benefit Analysis of Orbital Debris Remediation.* Washington, DC: NASA.

Office of Technology, Policy, and Strategy (2024). *Space-Based Solar Power.* Washington, DC: NASA.

Parsons Brinckerhoff (2014). *2014 California High-Speed Rail Benefit-Cost Analysis.* Sacramento, CA: California High-Speed Rail Authority.

Raiden, A. et al. (2019). *Social Value in Construction.* Abingdon: Routledge.

Rogers, P.J., Stevens, K., Boymal, J. (2009). Qualitative Cost-Benefit Evaluation of Complex, Emergent Programs. *Evaluation and Program Planning*, 32: 83–90.

Roland Berger (2022). *Space-Based Solar Power: Can it Help to Decarbonize Europe and Make it More Energy Resilient? A study conducted for the European Space Agency.* Retrieved on February 7, 2024 from www.rolandberger.com/en/Insights/Publications/Space-based-Solar-Power.html.

Siciliano, G. et al. (2016). Adapted Cost-Benefit Analysis Methodology for Innovative Railway Services. *European Transport Research Review*, 8(23).

Sinden, A. (2019). The Problem of Unquantified Benefits. *Environmental Law*, 49(1) 73–129.

Smith, R. (1997). Engines of Discovery: Scientific Instruments and the History of Astronomy and Planetary Science in the United States in the Twentieth Century. *Journal for the History of Astronomy*, (28)1.

Sound Transit (2015). *ST3 Regional High-Capacity Transit System Plan: Benefit-Cost Analysis Methodology Report.* Seattle, WA: Sound Transit.

Taks, M. et al. (2011). Economic Impact Analysis Versus Cost Benefit Analysis: The Case of a Medium-Sized Sport Event. *International Journal of Sport Finance*, 6(3): 187–203.

The Rockefeller Foundation. (2013). *City Resilience Index.* Retrieved on 24 February 2024 from https://www.rockefellerfoundation.org/report/city-resilience-index-2.

United Nations (2015). *Transforming Our World: The 2030 Agenda for Sustainable Development.* A/RES/70/1. New York: Division for Social Development Goals, United Nations Department of Economic and Social Affairs.

USGBC (2025). *Leadership in Energy and Environmental Design (LEED) Green Building Rating* SystemTM, version 5. Atlanta, GA: U.S Green Building Council.

Wise, R.M., et al. (2022). Pragmatic Cost-Benefit Analysis for Infrastructure Resilience. *Nature Climate Change*, 12: 881–883.

Yuyar, G. (2021). *Economic Assessment of Public Projects Through Cost-Benefit Analysis: A Case Study on Istanbul Eurasia Tunnel.* Masters Degree Thesis, Politecnico Milano, School of Architecture, Urban Planning, and Construction Engineering.

Zwikael, O., Chih, Y., and Meredith, J. (2018). Project Benefit Management: Setting Effective Target Benefits. *International Journal of Project Management*, 36: 650–658.

11

CLOSING COMMENTS

When it comes to planning, purely financial economic analysis measures are often used to yield a quantitative ranking of proposed scenarios. However, projects are more complex than that. Qualitative methods, as used in program evaluation, can be used to supplement traditional cost-benefit analysis, enabling the identification, consideration, and management of qualitative effects such as societal value, resilience, and sustainability. Similarly, quantitative methods, as used in financial and economic analysis, can be used to supplement traditional program evaluation, stating the value of benefits and facilitating funding decisions.

The use of "artificial intelligence" to ease the complexities of analysis is still some years distant. Output from such systems is only as good as the data sets upon which trends and subsequent predictions are based. Until there is a larger population of benefit quantification and costing studies from which to obtain data, perform comparisons, and build models, any such use of databases is limited. However, it is feasible at this point in time for computer models to be used to apply net present value and other feasibility calculations, which may ease the quantification effort for evaluation practitioners.

The author hopes this contribution to the body of knowledge for strategic project analysis will result in greater maturity in the methodologies used and better awareness of bias, incommensurability, and data sensitivity. Ultimately, a deeper understanding of the pitfalls and failures of quantitative and qualitative analysis and the benefits of closer cooperation between the professions of evaluation and economic analysis may lead to new developments in the practices of project forecasting and decision-making, resulting in better

DOI: 10.4324/9781003014928-12

investments and more beneficial project outcomes. The author is also optimistic that funding for and results from the identification and quantification of benefits and disbenefits related to the full definitions of sustainability and resilience will improve the analysis of major projects.

12

SOLUTION SETS

CHAPTER 1: WHAT IS COST-BENEFIT ANALYSIS?

1. What are some major differences between engineering economics and welfare economics?
   a. One is almost exclusively quantitative, and focused on financial profitability. The other is largely qualitative, and focused on societal initiatives.
2. Name five (5) entities (not already named) that might utilize engineering economics methods. Explain why.
   a. Sample answer: ExxonMobil (new petrochemical plant location, focus on profitability), Amgen (new pharmaceutical manufacturing facility location, focus on profitability), LACCD (lease vs buy property, focus on most effective use of funds), Hill International (corporate acquisitions, focus on profitability), Altamed (expansion, focus on profitability)
3. Name five (5) entities (not already named) that might utilize welfare economics methods. Explain why.
   a. Sample answer: NRAO (new telescope array, broader impacts), CA HSR (high speed rail, community impact), FTA (airport expansion, changes to travel patterns), City of Charlottesville (homeless shelter, community impact), US Government (policy development, national social value impact)
4. What type of investments might necessitate engineering economics analysis? Name five (5) and explain why.
   a. Sample answer: New equipment vs repair, lease vs buy, expansion, new construction, corporate acquisitions. All focus on profitability.

DOI: 10.4324/9781003014928-13

5. What type of investments might entail welfare economics analysis? Name five (5) and explain why.
   a. Sample answer: Policy development, infrastructure (science, research), infrastructure (water, power, sewer, emergency services, transportation), city services, humanitarian efforts. All have community and social value impact.
6. In your own words, explain the difference between a Pareto scenario and a Kaldor-Hicks scenario.
   a. One strives to achieve an ideal where there are no losers, the other recognizes there will always be trade-offs.
7. When you make decisions, are they typically based on cost and/or profit, soft benefits, or a combination thereof? Explain and provide two (2) examples.
   a. Sample answer: Cost (washing machine), a combination of cost and soft benefits/prestige (travel)

CHAPTER 2: ANALYSIS PLANNING

1. See Figure 2.1. Why might the analysis revert to step three? Explain.
   a. More information may have become available that might change the analysis outcome. An ex-post analysis may be required.
2. See Figure 2.1. Why might the analysis revert to step two? Explain.
   a. The analysis may have eliminated scenarios or the scope may have changed, such that more scenarios need to be developed and analyzed.
3. What is the difference between "do nothing" and "do minimum"? Explain in your own words.
   a. "Do nothing" implies no change from the status quo, but may include maintenance to do so."Do nothing" may be the deferral option. "Do minimum" means investing the fewest resources possible to achieve the objective, likely at the expense of benefits.
4. Explain why no two projects can ever be exactly the same. Provide an example.
   a. Even if the design for two projects is identical, there will always be differences in labor resources, local conditions,

time, and cost. Sample answer: Construction – different inflation and pricing, contractor, weather, ground conditions, possible differences in regulatory/permitting. Sample answer: Societal benefit – different population, inflation and pricing, possible political/cultural differences.

5. Consider a scenario in which you are purchasing tickets to a concert. What might be your WTP for each ticket? Consider a scenario in which you own the concert tickets and the concert is sold out. What might be your WTA to give up the tickets? Discuss the difference between your WTP and WTA for this scenario.
   a. Sample answer: I'm solidly in the $25–$50 range for tickets but will occasionally go higher (to a couple of hundred $) for a big name.
   b. Sample answer: While I would greatly prefer to be reimbursed at face value for the tickets, I would probably give them away for free. I don't have the experience or bandwidth to bother with third-party aftermarket sales and market, but I can understand the inclination to add markup and make a profit, especially for a sold-out show. That markup would be the difference between WTA and WTP.
6. Benefits are $10,000 and costs are $8,500. Demonstrate whether or not the project is economically feasible by using two different methods of calculation.
   a. $10,000 - $8,500 = $1,500 > 0
      $10,000/$8,500 = 1.18 > 1
      The project is economically feasible.
7. Benefits are $105,000, disbenefits are $25,000, and costs are $80,500. Demonstrate whether or not the project is economically feasible by using two different methods of calculation.
   a. $105,000 - $25,000 - $80,500 = -$500 < 0
      ($105,000 - $25,000)/$80,500 = 0.99 < 1
      The project is not economically feasible.
8. Discuss how you might identify potential costs, benefits, and disbenefits for a major sporting event such as the FIFA World Cup. Name at least five (5) and explain.
   a. Sample answer: Look to past (internal) projects, search online, find published research/studies and actual published data for similar (external) projects, ask stakeholders and

subject matter experts, hire consultants, outreach to other major cities who have hosted the same event for their original analysis/actual data/lessons learned, and brainstorming.

9. Why is analysis documentation important? Name at least five (5) ways it might be used in the future, and explain.
    a. Sample answer: Analysis documentation may be used to answer questions raised during the review process, write the report, support an updated analysis, assist with future similar projects, and support an audit or ex-post analysis.
10. Name ten (10) types of documentation that might be created or obtained during an analysis.
    a. Sample answer: Schedule, interview records, meeting minutes, emails, calculations, photographs, narrative, cost data, contact information, list of omissions or exclusions.

CHAPTER 3: STAKEHOLDERS

1. What methods might be used to identify stakeholders? Name at least five (5) and explain.
    a. Sample answer: Look to past (internal) projects, search online, find published research/studies and actual published data for similar (external) projects, ask subject matter experts, hire consultants, outreach to other entities with similar projects, community outreach, surveys, city records, geographic data and maps, relationship mapping, mindmapping, and brainstorming.
2. Identify fifteen (15) categories of stakeholders for a scenario in which a temporary field hospital is being established in another country.
    a. Sample answer: Patients, families of patients, local food suppliers, local material suppliers, international medical suppliers, nursing staff, doctor staff, administration staff, transportation crew, construction crew, maintenance staff, local government, Sample answer: local military, aid organizations, financial contributors.
3. What type of stakeholder obligations might be defined by a preexisting contract? Name at least five (5) and explain.
    a. Sample answer: Employment contracts (employer, work scope, quality), financing arrangements (funding, oversight),

procurement contracts (scope, requirements, pricing), consulting contracts (employer, work scope, pricing), acceptance of funds from taxes and bonds (implicit contract).

4. What type of stakeholder obligations might result from societal norms? Name at least five (5) and explain.
   a. Sample answer: Future generations, sustainability, equity, distributional effects, expectations of job creation, cooperation, inclusion, communication, assurance, cultural and religious sensitivity, political sensitivity.
5. What is the difference between assurance and accountability? Explain in your own words.
   a. Accountability means taking responsibility for one's actions or for the state of something for which one is accountable. Assurance means one is providing accurate and complete information to ease concerns and increase confidence in a situation. Assurance is an action of accountability.
6. How can an organization explicitly provide assurance to stakeholders? Name at least five (5) and explain.
   a. Sample answer: Regular communication, transparency, inclusion, cooperation, responsiveness.

CHAPTER 4: RISK

1. Name five (5) types of risk (not already named) that might be quantified using welfare economics methods. Explain why and how they might be quantified.
   a. Sample answer: Traffic (time, mileage, maintenance), pollution (carbon cost), accidents (repairs, medical treatment), job creation, staff retention (training, COBRA, vacation payout, wage differential), compliance (penalties)
2. Find three (3) examples of monetary proxy for societal benefits or disbenefits. Cite your sources.
   a. Sample answer:
      i. Value per statistical life (with link).
      ii. Emissions and environmental impacts (with link).
      iii. Electric power interruptions (with link).
3. Identify twenty (20) types of risk for a scenario in which a new pharmaceutical manufacturing plant is being constructed in Puerto Rico.

   a. Sample answer: Specialized construction labor, inflation, market forces, regulatory requirements, schedule acceleration, liquidated damages, weather, archaeological findings, utilities capacity, transportation infrastructure, permanent labor capacity, language barrier, productivity, smuggling, long lead equipment, materials theft, local government influence, concrete testing, local culture, shipping delays.
4. Using your own words, explain why sensitivity testing is a type of risk analysis.
   a. Sensitivity analysis tests the effect different variables have on the analysis output, and helps to identify critical variables such as the discount rate. It is a risk analysis of the accuracy of the analysis.
5. When you make decisions, how sensitive are you to risk? Explain and provide two (2) examples.
   a. Sample answer: I am sensitive to financial risk (investments), but not to personal risk (travel, sports).

CHAPTER 5: QUANTITATIVE CONCEPTS

1. If you invest $1,000 today at an interest rate of 8 percent per year, how much will the investment be worth in five years? Perform the calculation twice, once using the equation and once using Microsoft Excel.
   a. $F = P(1+i)^n = F = 1000(1.08)^5 = \$1,469.33$
   b. In MS Excel, the function for this is FV(0.08,5,,-1000)
2. Calculate the net present value for the scenario shown in Table 5.1 and Figure 5.1, at an interest rate of 5 percent per year.

Time (Years)	*Equipment Cost ($K)*	*Repair Cost ($K)*	*Revenue ($K)*	*Salvage Value ($K)*	*Present value, i=5%*
0 (Today)	-10,000	0	0	0	
1	0	-952	2,857	0	
2	0	-907	2,721	0	
3	0	-864	2,592	0	
4	0	-823	2,468	0	
5	0	-784	2,351	2,351	
					1,010

3. Draw a cash flow diagram for the following scenario:

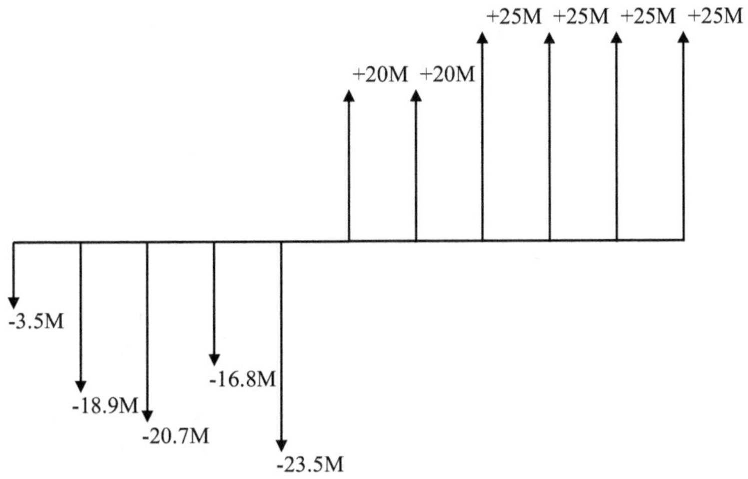

4. Find three (3) examples of different discount rates used in cost-benefit analyses. Cite your sources.
   a. Sample answer:
      i. Space-based solar power 10 percent (with link).
      ii. CA HSR 12% (with link).
      iii. Phoenix green infrastructure 3 percent (with link).
5. How might the future value equation be useful to you in real life? Provide two (2) examples.
   a. Sample answer: The future value equation can be used to calculate the value of an investment with a fixed interest rate (such as a bond purchase), or the value of one with an estimated rate of appreciation (such as a house).
6. How might the annuity payment equation be useful to you in real life? Provide two (2) examples.
   a. Sample answer: The annuity payment equation can be used to calculate the monthly payment on a car loan, or the number of years remaining to pay on a student loan.

CHAPTER 6: QUALITATIVE CONCEPTS

1. How might qualitative analysis methods be useful to you in real life? Provide two (2) examples.
    a. Sample answer: A pros and cons list or weighted decision matrix can be used for everyday decisions about purchases (refrigerator replacement) and actions (weekend activity selection).
2. Explain why a decision matrix might be used for scenario selection instead of a pros and cons list. Provide an example.
    a. Sample answer: A decision matrix allows weighting of criteria, whereas a pros and cons list does not. Where cost is of higher significance (stove/oven replacement), that element can be weighted. Where longevity is of higher significance (mattress replacement), that element can be weighted. It also enables scoring, yielding a quantitative result.
3. Find one published example each of a cost-effectiveness analysis, an objectives-based impact evaluation, and a value-for-money study. Cite your sources.
    a. Sample answer:
        i. Healthcare diabetes treatment, CEA (with link).
        ii. Housing charity VFM (with link)
        iii. SKA socioeconomic assessment (with link).
4. How might qualitative analysis be used to supplement the results obtained from an economic analysis? Provide an example, and explain how this might affect decision-making.
    a. Sample answer: A qualitative analysis or narrative that highlights soft benefits and difficult-to-price elements may influence decision-making toward a low-profit or uneconomic scenario. For example, science research facilities require significant investment but yield benefits such as education impact, development of new ideas and products, contributions to science and human knowledge, and more.
5. Explain in your own words why the use of an effectiveness measure or utility measure can be potentially problematic.
    a. Sample answer: Effectiveness and utility measures can be highly subjective, and variations in the measures can impact

the calculations (and, subsequently, scenario selection). One way to avoid such subjectivity would be to include input from multiple sources when developing the measures, such that the measures used represent an aggregate.

6. Explain in your own words how weighting might unfairly affect scenario selection.
   a. Sample answer: If decision-makers add weighting without fully analyzing the affected stakeholder groups, the relative importance of the elements being analyzed might not be truly representative and authentic. This can result in the selection of a scenario that might not otherwise have been chosen. Weighting, in its most damaging incarnation, is effectively the same as bias and may surface ethical issues with the analysis.

CHAPTER 7: PERSPECTIVE, BIAS, AND ETHICS

1. Find five (5) published examples of cost-benefit analysis, and identify the perspective used for each. Cite your sources.
   a. Sample answer:
      i. Space-based solar power, organizational perspective (with link).
      ii. CA HSR, organizational perspective, economic analysis with shadow pricing for social value and environmental benefits (with link).
      iii. Phoenix green infrastructure, organizational perspective, economic analysis with shadow pricing for social value and environmental benefits (with link).
      iv. NASA Orbital debris remediation, organizational perspective, economic analysis with shadow pricing for collision damage and risk (with link).
      v. Agricultural R&D, social perspective using an impact model (with link).
2. Is there a difference in perspective between engineering economics and welfare economics? Explain.
   a. There can be, yes. A purely financial/economic analysis will likely take an owner or investor's perspective, with focus on profitability and efficiency in resource use. Welfare economics more commonly takes a societal perspective,

focusing on societal or sustainability benefits instead of just monetary cost.

3. Identify five (5) types of cognitive bias that you recognize in yourself. The list of biases need not be restricted to those identified in the text above.
   a. Sample answer: Blind spot bias (viewing oneself as less biased than others), availability heuristic (accepting availability of information as a proxy for importance), hyperbolic discounting (choosing immediate gratification), post-purchase rationalization (retroactively justifying an action), risk compensation (risk tolerance increases when greater safety is perceived).
4. Are you bound by an ethics code? Consider all possible sources, including your employer, religion, culture, and any organizations of which you are a member. Explain.
   a. Sample answer: I am bound by at least ten ethics codes, the majority of which are professional institutions.
5. If you are subject to several ethics codes, consider the differences between them. Do the ethics codes conflict in any way? Explain and discuss.
   a. Sample answer: It is highly likely that my employer's ethics code and code of conduct conflict with that of my professional institutions, in terms of duty and fidelity. The professional institution ethics codes generally align with each other.
6. Describe a situation in which a scenario might be selected even though costs exceed benefits.
   a. Sample answer: Innovation departments require significant investment but yield benefits such as education impact, development of new ideas and products, contributions to science and human knowledge, and more. Costs are likely to exceed benefits for the first few years. Depending on the timeframe of analysis, the scenario might be selected even though costs exceed benefits.
7. Explain in your own words how lobbying and political influence might affect the outcome of an analysis.
   a. If the analysis is financed and/or conducted by a lobbying group or political party, it may be conducted from the perspective of that entity.

b. Cognitive biases such as the availability heuristic (perceiving increased importance of something because it is readily available/being broadcasted aggressively), the bandwagon effect (perceiving increased importance of something because others are endorsing it), belief bias (accepting something because it is believable even though the argument is not sound) might all occur and cause the analysis to reflect a certain perspective as a result of lobbying and political influence.
c. Conversely, reactive devaluation (discounting a concept because it came from an adversary or opponent), and stereotyping (attributing characteristics to something because it came from a certain group) might also occur and cause the analysis to reflect an opposing perspective as a result of lobbying and political involvement.

CHAPTER 8: REVIEWING AN ANALYSIS REPORT

1. Find two (2) published examples of quantitative or qualitative strategic project analysis. Identify the funding source, perspective, objective, intended audience, and intended use for each. Cite your sources.
   a. Sample answer:
      i. CA HSR, CA HSR, organizational perspective, economic justification, general public, CA HSR business plan (with link).
      ii. Group Work/JOBS II, fellowship funding from Health Foundation, organizational perspective, test of effectiveness of the intervention, DWP, future use of the course (with link).
2. Find two (2) published examples of quantitative cost-benefit analysis. Try to duplicate the mathematical calculations. Does the report contain sufficient information for you to do so? Why or why not? Cite your sources.
   a. Sample answer:
      i. Bolu Mountain Tunnel, equations are shown and described, cost data is shown, calculation methodology is explained, maths can be duplicated (with link).
      ii. Space shuttle program, some data is shown and described, equations not shown, supplementary report

referenced but not provided, maths could not be duplicated (with link).

3. Find two (2) published examples of quantitative or qualitative strategic project analysis. Are the tables and figures easy to understand, does the report provide an adequate amount of detail, and does the executive summary correctly represent the detailed conclusions of the report? Why or why not? Cite your sources.
   a. Sample answer:
      i. NASA space-based solar power, excellent tables and figures, good amount of detail and discussion of methodology and model, assumptions explained, executive summary matches conclusion (with link).
      ii. ST3, good tables and figures, assumptions explained, detailed discussion of methodology and data, no executive summary provided (with link).
4. Find three (3) published examples, one each of a qualitative, a quantitative, and a blended-approach strategic project analysis. Review the reports critically, and write a two-page reviewer's summary per report. Identify the context, discuss any issues identified, and suggest improvements. Cite your sources.
   a. (Exercise)
5. Write five (5) questions to supplement the critical questioning section above.
   a. Sample answer:
      i. Does the report reference other supplementary reports?
      ii. How does the report treat disbenefits?
      iii. Is the report redacted for a specific audience?
      iv. Can the maths be replicated?
      v. How does the report treat risk?

CHAPTER 9: SUSTAINABILITY AND RESILIENCE

1. Explain in your own words how sustainability and resilience overlap. Provide two (2) examples not already mentioned.
   a. Sample answer: Both frameworks address social value concepts.
   b. Sample answer:
      i. The provision of services and resources such as such as food, health, education, water and sanitation, energy, and safety.
      ii. Robust economic growth and balanced ecosystems.

2. Explain in your own words where sustainability and resilience diverge. Provide two (2) examples not already mentioned.
   a. Sample answer: The difference is in the emphasis of certain concepts. Resilience accentuates infrastructure, whereas sustainability highlights the environment and overall well-being.
   b. Sample answer:
      i. The Rockefeller goals mention building planning and codes, hazard mapping, and redundant capacity).
      ii. The Rockefeller goals consider housing and transportation, but the UN goals do not.
3. What types of sustainability benefits and disbenefits might be difficult to quantify? Explain.
   a. Sample answer: Well-being seems subjective as a concept, and the benefits of gender equality and empowerment are vague. "Decent work" is ill-defined.
4. What types of resilience benefits and disbenefits might be difficult to quantify? Explain.
   a. Sample answer: The benefits of strong identity and culture are not described.
5. Can you identify any additional societal value benefits that are not listed in the sustainability and resilience goals? Explain.
   a. Sample answer: Efficiency of planning approvals, equitable city planning, accessibility, smart cities, terrorism and war.

CHAPTER 10: SCENARIOS

1. Explain in your own words why costs, benefits, and disbenefits are difficult to identify and quantify for unique projects. Provide two (2) examples not already mentioned.
   a. If a project has never before been done, there will likely be many unknown costs that require creative estimating. The project may require specialty equipment and materials, which are also difficult to cost (in estimating, we sometimes refer to a rare or specialty material as "unobtanium"). Any disbenefits and benefits may be difficult to forecast if the impacts are not intuitively comparable to other projects in a similar category. Some unique projects may need to be in operation for a longer timeframe before benefits and disbenefits appear, in which case they

might not be included (or may be heavily discounted) in the analysis.

   b. Sample answer: Example 1: A chemical process plant that uses new technology and specialized materials. Example 2: Almost every non-earth-based space science project.

2. List thirty-five (35) categories of potential costs, benefits, and disbenefits for a new toll road.
   a. Sample answer: Construction costs (materials, construction labor, onsite and offsite management, equipment, contractor and subcontractors, consultants, permits, insurance, taxes, financing costs, field office, utilities), land acquisition, operation costs (operations labor, scheduled maintenance, management, utilities, insurance, unscheduled maintenance).
   b. Sample answer: Operations revenue (tolls, advertising).
   c. Sample answer: Benefits (reduced accidents, reduced injuries, reduced fatalities, reduced traffic, shorter travel time, job creation).
   d. Sample answer: Disbenefits (increased noise, lost green space, impact to wildlife, stormwater pollution, light pollution, increased carbon emissions).
3. What types of costs, benefits, and disbenefits might be identified for a privatized space science project in an ex-post analysis, but not in an ex-ante analysis? Explain.
   a. Sample answer: In the ex-post analysis, additional long-term benefits and disbenefits will be identified for the project such as space waste, air pollution, radiation, astronaut health impacts, higher risk, quality issues, and actual innovation revenue (licensing, manufacturing, patents) can be added.
   b. Sample answer: Actual construction and maintenance costs can also be added to the ex-post analysis, fine-tuning the original estimates.
4. Identify some recent legislation or societal initiative that has affected you. Identify, explain, and quantify the impacts to yourself.
   a. Sample answer: Recent property tax increases to fund community college construction – cost (cost of the tax increase at $22 per $100,000 of assessed property value), disbenefits (lack of tax funding for other initiatives, increased

pedestrian and vehicle traffic, increased noise, impact on parking, increased light pollution, slight increase in crime), benefits (community use of the library and sports facilities, more theatre and music events).

b. Sample answer: Local smart city initiative – cost (none), benefits (more tech businesses and jobs, climate action plan, new city office of sustainability, expanded IoT, open data portal, technology development and innovation, procurement opportunities, smart grid power network), disbenefits (long time required for implementation and innovation, geographic inequity, lack of expansion to County).

5. Identify a recent construction project that is local to you. Identify, explain, and quantify the impacts to yourself.

A. Sample answer: Construction of a neighbor's house – temporary disbenefits (increased traffic, increased noise, increased dust and dirt, lawn damage by construction vehicle), permanent disbenefits (loss of scenic view, loss of privacy, increased noise, loss of green space, loss of unofficial parking area), potential benefits (new neighbors, more parties and societal opportunities, new neighborhood dog). No cost impact.

INDEX

Note: Page numbers in *italics* refer to figures.

For Product Safety Concerns and Information please contact our EU
representative GPSR@taylorandfrancis.com
Taylor & Francis Verlag GmbH, Kaufingerstraße 24, 80331 München, Germany

www.ingramcontent.com/pod-product-compliance
Lightning Source LLC
LaVergne TN
LVHW021130300926
849160LV00010B/950

9781032874500